A Source Book
of Twentieth-Century Warships

A Source Book of
Twentieth-Century Warships

Written and compiled by
Michael Janitch

WARD LOCK LIMITED · LONDON

© Ward Lock Limited 1977

ISBN 0 7063 1819 6

First published in Great Britain 1977
by Ward Lock Limited, 116 Baker Street,
London, W1M 2BB, a member of the Pentos Group

Text filmset in Univers (685)

Printed and bound in Great Britain by
Cox & Wyman Ltd,
London, Fakenham and Reading

Frontispiece picture:
USS *Brooklyn*, armoured cruiser of 1896, a type of ship that
ranked second only to the battleship. She represents the state
of the art to which naval architecture had aspired by the turn
of the century

Preface

The subject 'twentieth-century warships' covers a vast panorama, and it would be wholly unrealistic to imagine that a theme of such immensity and complexity could be covered here in depth. However, I have attempted to give a general outline of the evolution of the five main categories of surface warship — Capital ships (Battleships and Battle-cruisers), Aircraft carriers, Cruisers, Destroyers and Escorts — produced by the world's major ship-building countries.

Wherever possible, pictures depict a ship soon after completion, or at least in her original state, although in some unavoidable cases vessels are portrayed after having undergone some major refit or modernization.

Submarines have been excluded from this book on the basis that this type of vessel is an entity in its own right, with different origins from those of surface ships. Indeed it is only within the last twenty years that the submarine has acquired the status of 'ship', since the advent of nuclear-powered, ballistic-missile-firing submarines, before which it was regarded as an underwater torpedo 'boat'. But if for no better reason, submersible craft should be excluded on the basis subscribed to by a then future First Sea Lord, Admiral Sir A. K. Wilson, who described the submarine during the early part of this century as being 'underhand, unfair and damned un-English'!

Michael Janitch

Introduction

The year 1900 is purely an arbitrary one for the commencing date of this book, chosen for its calendar significance rather than to mark any great revolution in naval technology or architecture. It is therefore desirable to see how the warship had evolved prior to the beginning of the twentieth century, in order to have a firm foundation on which to work.

The Battleship

In the first half of the nineteenth century the first-rate ship-of-the-line, upon whose numbers the comparative strength of a maritime nation was assessed, had changed little from those men-of-war that had defeated the great Spanish Armada in 1588. Indeed, so slowly had warship design developed during the intervening years that Nelson's flagship, HMS *Victory*, was more than forty years old at the Battle of Trafalgar in 1805, although she was still considered to be one of the most powerful ships in the British fleet.

However, all this changed once the benefits of the Industrial Revolution had started to be applied to naval construction from about the 1850s, and these were to transform the appearance of the fighting ship beyond all recognition. The steam engine replaced sail as the main source of motive power; iron and then steel became the primary building materials in place of wood; and the breach-loading, rifled, shell-firing gun contained within a turret displaced the muzzle-loading, smooth-bore cannon, which had been sited in great profusion on a vessel's broadside and fired solid projectiles. This period also saw the inception and development of the torpedo, whose influence on naval warfare was to be so dramatic.

One innovation followed another, requiring the constant reappraisal of warship design, and so rapid were the advancements in naval technology and architecture that capital ships were to become obsolete even while they were still under construction. Nevertheless, many new design features were speculative, and it was a moot point whether armament, armour protection, speed or endurance should be treated as the top design priority for new construction.

Also in question was how naval strategy and tactics should be conducted so as to obtain the maximum benefit from the possession of such novel maritime hardware. These uncertainties arose because up until the early 1900s, there had been no major action between the opposing fleets of two well-equipped navies since the Battle of Trafalgar, nearly one hundred years before.

It was not until the Russo–Japanese War of 1904–5 that modern warships could be tested under true combat conditions and lessons could therefore be learned to provide information for future construction. The War started in February 1904, when Japanese torpedo boats launched a pre-emptive attack on the Russian Far Eastern Squadron while it was at anchor in Port Arthur harbour, Manchuria. This, however, achieved relatively little success: only minor damage was caused to two battleships and a cruiser and this

Italian torpedo boat, *circa* 1900, not unlike the Japanese craft that attacked the Russian fleet in Port Arthur in February 1904

result perpetuated the myth in certain quarters that the battleship was virtually invulnerable to this form of attack, especially when at sea, travelling at speed and able to take evasive action. Later in the war mines were to prove their worth, although they remained somewhat unreliable. But it was the ensuing Battle of Tsushima, when Admiral Togo's Squadron annihilated the Russian Baltic Fleet on its arrival in the Sea of Japan in May 1905, that confirmed the heavy shell as the arbitrary factor in a naval action.

Tsushima was, however, the last sea battle to be fought using traditional gunnery techniques, which were unchanged since Nelson's day, whereby each gunlayer was responsible for aiming and firing his own weapon, thus limiting the accurate range of a maritime encounter to about 3,000 yards (although 12-in guns could fire their shells to far greater distances). But latterly, in order to increase battle ranges, a system had been devised that enabled the entire battery of heavy guns to be controlled from a centralized position carried aloft, well above any interference from spray or smoke. From there, salvoes (that is, half the guns fired simultaneously) could be co-ordinated and the fall of shot observed in relation to the target. Corrections in range and/or bearing could then be determined and transmitted to the gun crews, who would make the necessary adjustments in elevation and/or training.

But with battleships now mounting guns of two or three different calibres (an intermediate battery had been added in newer ships to increase the weight of a broadside) spotting became a nightmare. This was because it was impossible to differentiate between splashes created by different sizes of shell whose guns had varied rates of fire according to calibre, and required different degrees of elevation to achieve the same range, resulting in varied trajectories for different periods of flight-time.

The answer was the uniform calibre armament, or the all-big-gun battleship, which first materialized in the form of HMS *Dreadnought* in 1906, built in the record time of 366 days. So revolutionary was her design that she instantly rendered every other battleship in the world obsolete, and was the archetype of a new class of warship to which she gave her name. Unfortunately, she had the long-term effect of devaluing Britain's own supremacy in capital ships (in which she outnumbered the combined fleets of any other two navies), as other nations soon started to build dreadnoughts. This situation sparked off an intense

HMS *Dreadnought*, 18,110 tons, the first all-big-gun
battleship, was built in the record time of 366 days

naval arms race between Great Britain and Germany, which culminated in August 1914 with the former having forty-two and the latter twenty-seven dreadnought-type battleships and battle-cruisers either built or under construction.

After the signing of the Armistice in November 1918 the war-impoverished nations of Europe had little money left for the construction of battleships. With the major part of the Kaiserliche Marine's High Seas Fleet at the bottom of Scapa Flow (after its self-imposed destruction in June 1919) and the Treaty of Versailles (signed June 1919), which limited Germany to a token navy suitable only for a coastal-defence role, the sole threat to Britain's maritime supremacy in Europe was removed. However, since the war a new ship-building contest had been gathering momentum between the United States and Japan for command of the Pacific. Both countries embarked on massive naval programmes, each calling for the construction of sixteen capital ships. The largest of these would have displaced nearly 50,000 tons, and mounted 18-in guns. The United Kingdom was, therefore, compelled to reciprocate in 1921 by ordering four 48,000-ton battle-cruisers armed with 16-in guns, and made known her intention to build eight battleships of similar displacement mounting 18-in guns. This intense and expensive rivalry had to be brought to a halt before all the participants faced financial ruin.

At the invitation of President Harding, the former wartime allies convened at a conference held in Washington in November 1921. The resultant naval-limitation treaty was signed the following February. This brought about the abandonment of the major part of the American and Japanese programmes, and the cancellation of Britain's twelve projected capital ships. In addition Britain accepted parity with the United States in numbers of capital ships by scrapping about twenty of her older units; Japan was permitted to retain three capital ships for every five possessed by each of the two major sea powers, while France and Italy were each allowed a ratio of 1.75 on the same basis.

No further capital ships were to be laid down for a period of ten years, except the British battleships *Nelson* and *Rodney*, to compensate for the 16-in-gunned units of the American Maryland and Japanese Nagato classes. This was subsequently extended to fifteen years (first London Naval Treaty of 1930) by Great Britain, the United States and Japan, who further reduced their respective battle fleets to 15, 15 and 9 units. Thereafter, each vessel could be replaced on reaching twenty years of age. New construction, however, should not exceed 35,000 tons (standard) displacement, and carry guns in excess of 16-in in calibre. The 5:5:3:1.75:1.75 Treaty ratio would therefore yield aggregate tonnages of 525,000 for both Britain and the USA, 315,000 for Japan, and 175,000 for both France and Italy, when all original units had been replaced.

During the inter-war years, many World War I veteran battleships were modernized, almost to the point of total reconstruction. Particular emphasis was paid to improving horizontal and underwater protection, and to the provision of

HMS *Valiant*, 31,100 tons, completed in 1916, was twice modernized between the wars, in 1929–30 (as shown) and again in 1937–9

anti-aircraft guns, although the Washington Treaty prohibited a vessel's displacement being increased by more than 3,000 tons when rejuvenated.

At the close of 1934 Japan gave the statutory two-year notice of her intention to withdraw from the obligations of the Washington Treaty, which would thus be automatically terminated on the last day of December 1936. After Germany's new Head of State, Adolf Hitler, publicly renounced the Treaty of Versailles and committed his country to a programme of rearmament, Great Britain reached a bilateral treaty with Germany in June 1935, which permitted the Kriegsmarine to build up to 35 per cent of the total tonnage of the Royal Navy in all categories of surface vessel. However, only a tacit understanding existed that German battleships should not exceed 35,000 tons, and this was not ratified until qualitative limitations were imposed retrospectively in 1937 (corresponding with those of the first London Naval Treaty). In the interim *Bismarck* and *Tirpitz* had been laid down to a design greatly exceeding the figure specified.

Representatives of the five original signatory powers to the Washington Treaty assembled in London in December 1935 to thrash out a new agreement to take effect from 1 January, 1937.

The resultant treaty bore only the signatures of the delegates from the United Kingdom (and British Dominions), United States and France. This perpetuated the 35,000-ton limit on battleships for a further six years, although this was subsequently increased to 45,000 tons in 1938. There was also a tentative proposal to reduce the maximum calibre of gun borne by future capital ships to 14 in, if all five original signatories to the Washington Treaty were to agree to this. However, no such unanimity was forthcoming and the 16-in gun was retained as the upper limit.

In September 1939 the comparative strengths in capital ships of the main belligerent powers, that is, three Allied and three Axis powers, were:

	In service	Under construction	On order
Great Britain	15	7	2
United States	15	4	2
France	7	3	1
Germany	2	4	7
Italy	4	4	0
Japan	10	2	2

Although at the time the offensive capabilities of the aircraft carrier were certainly appreciated, the battleship entered World War II still 'Queen of the Seas', but events were slowly to erode her status as the capital ship of a fleet. Carrier-borne aircraft achieved two notable successes against battleships early in the war, when three Italian units were disabled in Taranto harbour by aircraft from HMS *Illustrious* in November 1940, and again thirteen months later, when the Japanese launched an aerial attack from a six-carrier task force on the American Pacific Fleet in Pearl

HMS *Illustrious*, 23,000 tons, whose aircraft carried out the very successful attack on the Italian fleet in Taranto harbour in November 1940

Harbor, which included eight battleships. Half these were sunk, while the remainder were damaged to varying degrees. But it was the loss of HMS *Prince of Wales* and her consort, the battle-cruiser *Repulse*, to Japanese shore-based aircraft in December 1941 (three days after Pearl Harbor), which sounded the death knell of the battleship. The *Prince of Wales* was a new ship, incorporating a strong armoured deck against bomb hits and intricate subdivision of the hull to nullify the impact of torpedo explosions, while mounting a comparatively efficient battery of AA guns. But still she succumbed, although steaming at high speed and able to take evasive action.

HMS *Prince of Wales*, 36,750 tons, was sunk in the South China Sea by Japanese aircraft in December 1941

After her loss no country ordered further battleships.

Battleships went on to perform valuable service for the remainder of World War II, screening fast carrier task forces with their vast batteries of light AA guns, and bombarding invasion objectives in support of amphibious assault operations. At the time of writing (1977), apart from a few that have been preserved as memorials, only the four battleships of the American Iowa class remain in existence out of the 175 or so dreadnought-type vessels that had been built for the world's navies over a period of fifty years. The Iowas themselves are now all out of commission and laid up with the Reserve Fleet, though all fought in the Korean War of 1950–3 and one, the *New Jersey*, was reactivated for the Vietnam War to be used in the fire-support role. But she too is now back in 'mothballs'.

USS *Wisconsin*, 48,500 tons, is one of the four surviving battleships of the Iowa class

Notes on Data and Abbreviations

Abbreviations for the nationalities of the ships listed:
GB = Great Britain, USA = United States of America, USSR = the Soviet Union, D = Germany, F = France, I = Italy, J = Japan, C = Canada, N = Netherlands, NZ = New Zealand. The year quoted at the head of each entry refers to the vessel's launch date, or the date of conversion.

The statistical data is arranged as follows:

Built: *The name of the shipbuilder;* the *geographical location* of the yard; and the *period of construction* (from keel laying to completion).

Dimensions: Three figures are given: the overall length (from stem to stern); the maximum width of the hull (or in some cases its waterline measurement); and the mean draught; the displacement (weight of water displaced by the bulk of the ship) is given in Imperial tons.

Armament: The number and calibre of guns carried (their function: LA and HA for use against surface targets, DP and AA); number and calibre of torpedo tubes; the number of aircraft carried (with their associated equipment). Where a missile armament is shipped, the type of launcher is quoted (whether single or multiple) with the name of the weapon system and its function (SAM, SSM or ASM). Wherever possible, the maximum number of depth charges that can be carried is stated, with their launch devices (throwers or stern rails). Where a DCM is borne, the presentation usually follows that for guided-missile launchers.

Machinery: Number of shafts (indicating the number of propellers); the type of propulsion system; the designed maximum or best-achieved horse-power figure; the speed attained by this at mean draught. Where steam is generated as the main power source for machinery, the number of boilers or nuclear reactors is quoted.

Fuel: The maximum capacity, either of coal or oil or both.

Radius: The endurance achieved with the above bunkerage while steaming at a stated speed, measured in nautical miles (6,080 feet).

Armour: Maximum thickness of armour applied to the sides (belt) and deck (usually placed directly over the magazines). The figure quoted for the main turrets applies to the turret faces where protection is at its thickest.

Crew: Usually the peace-time complement.

Abbreviations

AA	Anti-Aircraft
AP	Armour-Piercing
AS	Anti-Submarine
Asdic	Allied Submarine Detection Investigation Committee
ASM	Anti-Submarine Missile
Asroc	Anti-Submarine Rocket
ASW	Anti-Submarine Weapon
BPDMS	Basic Point Defence Missile System
COGOG	Combined Gas turbine or Gas turbine machinery
COSAG	Combined Steam and Gas turbine machinery
DC	Depth Charge
DCM	Depth Charge Mortar
DCT	Depth Charge Thrower
DP	Dual Purpose
FAA	Fleet Air Arm
fd	flight deck
HA	High Angle
IJN	Imperial Japanese Navy
LA	Low Angle
LAMPS	Light Airborne Multi-Purpose System
N.Yd	Navy Yard
NATO	North Atlantic Treaty Organization
pdr	pounder
RAN	Royal Australian Navy
RCN	Royal Canadian Navy
RIN	Royal Indian Navy
RN	Royal Navy
RNZN	Royal New Zealand Navy
SAM	Ship-to-Air Missile
SONAR	Sound Navigation and Ranging (formerly Asdic)
SSM	Ship-to-Surface Missile
TT	Torpedo Tube
VDS	Variable Depth Sonar
VTE	Vertical Triple Expansion engine
VTOL	Vertical Take-Off and Landing aircraft
WWI	World War I
WWII	World War II

Hogue (GB) 1900

Seen here in Victorian livery, *Hogue* was one of six armoured cruisers of the Cressy class built for completion in 1901–3, to counter the large and powerful cruisers that were being completed for the French Navy with alarming regularity. These were the first armoured cruisers (the term denotes an armour belt carried at the waterline) to be built for the RN for more than a decade. In the interim first-class protected cruisers were constructed, which relied upon a steel deck placed below the waterline over the ship's vitals to resist shellfire. However, the new steel armour plate, recently developed by Krupps, proved infinitely tougher than the old compound armour, and therefore required a thinner belt to resist 6-in shells.

In September 1914 *Hogue* and her two sister ships, *Aboukir* and *Cressy*, were sunk in the North Sea by the German submarine *U.9*. The three survivors of the class, *Bacchante*, *Euryalus* and *Sutlej*, were sold for scrap in 1920.

Built: Vickers, Barrow (July 1898–1902).
Dimensions: 472×69½×25 ft = 12,000 tons
Armament: 2 9.2-in (LA), 12 6-in (LA), 14 12-pdr (LA) guns; 2 18-in (submerged) TTs.

Machinery: 2-shaft reciprocating (VTE), 21,000 hp = 21 kts. **Boilers:** 30. **Fuel:** 1,600 tons coal. **Armour:** belt 6 in, turrets 6 in, deck 3 in. **Crew:** 760

Mikasa (J) 1900

Typical of battleship design at the turn of the century, armed with four big guns in twin turrets fore and aft, a quick-firing medium calibre battery, disposed equally (usually in casemates) on either broadside, and a tertiary battery for anti-torpedo boat defence. Built in the United Kingdom to a design similar to that of contemporary British battleships, *Mikasa* was the flagship of Vice-Admiral Heihachiro Togo's combined fleet throughout the Russo–Japanese War of 1904–5, and the venue of the Russian-surrender ceremony. Relegated to second-line duties, but was retained as an active unit during WWI. Now preserved to commemorate Admiral Togo's decisive victory over the Russian Baltic Fleet at the Battle of Tsushima.

Built: Vickers, Barrow (Jan. 1899–Mar. 1902).
Dimensions: 432×75½×27 ft = 15,140 tons.
Armament: 4 12-in (LA), 14 6-in (LA), 20 12-pdr (LA) guns; 4 18-in (submerged) TTs.
Machinery: 2-shaft reciprocating (VTE), 15,000 hp = 18 kts. **Boilers:** 25. **Fuel:** 1,520 tons coal.
Radius: 5,300 mls at 10 kts. **Armour:** belt 9 in, turrets 10 in, deck 3 in. **Crew:** 830

Dominion (GB) 1903

One of eight battleships belonging to the King Edward VII class to be completed during 1905–7, which were the first British vessels to mount an intermediate battery in addition to the 12-in and 6-in armament. This comprised four 9.2-in guns — each firing 380-lb projectiles — disposed in single turrets, two on each side, abreast the fore and mainmasts. The main and secondary batteries discharged shells weighing 850 lb and 100 lb respectively.

Other units of the class were: *King Edward VII, Commonwealth, New Zealand, Hindustan, Britannia, Africa* and *Hibernia. Dominion* was sold for scrap in 1921.

Built: Vickers, Barrow (May 1902–July 1905). **Dimensions:** $453\frac{3}{4} \times 78 \times 24\frac{1}{2}$ ft = 16,350 tons. **Armament:** 4 12-in (LA), 4 9.2-in (LA), 10 6-in (LA), 14 12-pdr (LA) guns; 4 18-in (submerged) TTs. **Machinery:** 2-shaft reciprocating (VTE), 18,000 hp = $18\frac{1}{2}$ kts. **Boilers:** 16. **Fuel:** 2,200 tons coal+380 tons oil. **Radius:** 7,000/3,150 mls at 10/17 kts. **Armour:** belt 9 in, turrets 12 in (main), 9 in (wing), deck $2\frac{1}{2}$ in. **Crew:** 777

Dreadnought (GB) 1906

The prototype all-big-gun battleship, armed with a single calibre main armament to facilitate fire control. The primary battery was carried in twin turrets, three on the centreline — one forward and two aft — and one on each side, forward of amidships. This allowed for an eight-gun broadside, equal to 6,800 lb, on either beam, the optimum number for salvo firing when range finding.

She was the first battleship to be fitted with turbine machinery, a far simpler and more reliable form of propulsion than the reciprocating engine it replaced, which offered a 3-knot-speed advantage over her contemporaries.

She was scrapped in 1923.

Built: HM Dockyard, Portsmouth (Oct. 1905– Oct. 1906). **Dimensions:** 526×82×26½ ft = 18,110 tons. **Armament:** 10 12-in (LA), 27 12-pdr (LA) guns; 5 18-in (submerged) TTs. **Machinery:** 4-shaft steam turbines, 23,000 hp = 21 kts. **Boilers:** 18. **Fuel:** 2,900 tons coal+1,120 tons oil. **Radius:** 6,620/4,910 mls at 10/18½ kts. **Armour:** belt 11 in, turrets 11 in, deck 2¾ in. **Crew:** 695–773

Scharnhorst   (D)   1906

With her sister ship *Gneisenau*, this was the most successful of all German armoured cruisers. Renowned for excellent shooting, they won the Kaiserliche Marine's top gunnery award (the Battle Practice Cup) for two successive years.

Scharnhorst was the flagship of Vice-Admiral Count von Spee's East Asiatic Squadron which sank the British armoured cruisers *Good Hope* and *Monmouth* at the Battle of Coronel in November 1914. There were no survivors from either ship, whose combined complement numbered some 1,600 men, including Rear-Admiral Sir Christopher Cradock. The loss of these two vessels was quickly avenged, as the battle-cruisers *Invincible* and *Inflexible* were promptly dispatched from the UK to the Falkland Islands, where it was correctly anticipated the German ships would next appear. There, in December 1914, after a long chase and great expenditure of ammunition, the *Scharnhorst* was sunk with no survivors, closely to be followed by the *Gneisenau*.

Built: Blohm & Voss, Hamburg (1905–7). **Dimensions:** $474\frac{1}{2} \times 71 \times 24\frac{1}{2}$ ft = 11,600 tons. **Armament:** 8 8.2-in (LA), 6 5.9-in (LA), 20 3.4-in (LA) guns; 4 17.7-in (submerged) TTs. **Machinery:** 3-shaft reciprocating (VTE), 26,000 hp = $22\frac{1}{2}$ kts. **Boilers:** 18. **Fuel:** 2,000 tons coal + 200 tons oil. **Armour:** belt 6 in, turrets 6 in, deck 2 in. **Crew:** 850

Invincible (GB) 1907

This ship had the same effect upon armoured-cruiser construction as did the *Dreadnought* on battleship design, by incorporating the same innovations: a single calibre main armament (of battleship proportions) and turbine propulsion. *Invincible* was preceded into service by sister ships *Inflexible* and *Indomitable*, and this class and its successors subsequently became known as battle-cruisers. Designed to reconnoitre ahead of the battle fleet, and if encountered, to sink the enemy's own reconnaissance cruisers, these ships were also intended to protect Britain's trade routes against commerce raiders. However, their powerful 12-in battery resulted in these ships being thought suitable to lie in the line of battle, despite the inability of their armour to resist heavy shell-fire. In effect, this altered their original design concept from that of the heavily armed cruiser to the lightly armoured battleship, or battle-cruiser.

Invincible was sunk at Jutland, May 1916.

Built: Armstrong Whitworth, Elswick (Apr. '06–Mar. '08). **Dimensions:** 567×78½×26¼ ft = 17,370 tons. **Armament:** 8 12-in (LA), 16 4-in (LA) guns; 5 18-in (submerged) TTs. **Machinery:** 4-shaft steam turbines, 44,875 hp = 26¼ kts. **Boilers:** 31. **Fuel:** 3,084 tons coal+725 tons oil. **Radius:** 3,050 mls at 23 kts. **Armour:** belt 6 in, turrets 7 in, deck 2½ in. **Crew:** 784

Michigan (USA) 1908

Together with sister ship *South Carolina*, she was the initial American interpretation of the all-big-gun battleship concept. Although their design pre-dated that of HMS *Dreadnought*, they were not laid down until after that ship's completion. Thereafter, construction was advanced at a leisurely pace. The disposition of the main armament was superior to that of the British vessel. All four 12-in turrets were carried on the centreline, with the inner pair superimposed over the other two, thus retaining a full eight-gun broadside, but mounting one less 600-ton turret.

The first ships to be completed with cagemasts (a distinctive feature peculiar to American capital ships for many years), which were thought to be shock absorbent and have unprecedented structural strength. However, the soundness of this theory came into question when *Michigan*'s foremast fell during a gale in 1918.

Built: New York Sbdg, New Jersey (Dec. '06–Jan. '10). **Dimensions:** $452\frac{3}{4} \times 80\frac{1}{4} \times 24\frac{1}{2}$ ft = 16,000 tons. **Armament:** 8 12-in (LA), 22 3-in (LA) guns; 2 21-in (submerged) TTs. **Machinery:** 2-shaft reciprocating (VTE), 16,500 hp = $18\frac{1}{2}$ kts. **Boilers:** 12. **Fuel:** 2,380 tons coal. **Radius:** 5,000 mls at 10 kts. **Armour:** belt 12 in, turrets 12 in, deck 3 in. **Crew:** 869

Nubian (GB) 1909

One of twelve Tribal class destroyers launched between 1907–9, which were almost double the size of their immediate predecessors, and the finest British oil-burning destroyers.

While remaining within Admiralty specifications, individual builders were given a high degree of latitude in the design of these vessels, which resulted in a very heterogeneous class.

In October 1916 *Nubian* was torpedoed by a German destroyer, which severely damaged her bow, and days later a sister ship, *Zulu*, had her stern blown off by a mine. Both wrecks were towed to Chatham, where the forward section of *Zulu* was attached to the after portion of *Nubian*. The resultant vessel, appropriately named *Zubian*, was commissioned in June 1917, and went on to win three battle honours and sink a German submarine. She was sold for scrap in 1919.

Built: Thornycroft, Southampton (1907–9). **Dimensions:** 280 × 26¾ × 9¾ ft = 998 tons. **Armament:** 2 4-in (LA) guns; 2 18-in (single) TTs. **Machinery:** 3-shaft steam turbines, 15,500 hp = 34 kts. **Boilers:** 5. **Fuel:** 216 tons oil. **Radius:** 2,350 mls at 15 kts. **Crew:** 72

Von der Tann   (D)   1909

First German battle-cruiser, and the Kaiserliche Marine's first major warship to have turbine propulsion and quadruple screws. Built as a reply to the British Invincible class, but with greater emphasis on armour protection and internal subdivision, as opposed to speed and armament. However, in the latter two cases she proved only marginally inferior to her British counterparts. The disposition of the main armament was similar to that in British battle-cruisers; four twin turrets, one forward, one aft, and one on each side amidships. The wing turrets were arranged in echelon to permit cross-deck firing for an eight-gun broadside. By pressing her boilers on trials, she achieved 79,000 hp for a speed of 27½ kts.

At Jutland she sank the battle-cruiser HMS *Indefatigable*. Scuttled at Scapa Flow in 1918.

Built: Blohm & Voss, Hamburg (Mar. '08–Sep. '10). **Dimensions:** $562\frac{2}{3} \times 87\frac{1}{4} \times 27\frac{1}{2}$ ft = 19,100 tons. **Armament:** 8 11-in (LA), 10 5.9-in (LA), 16 3.4-in (LA) guns; 4 17.7-in (submerged) TTs. **Machinery:** 4-shaft steam turbines, 42,000 hp = $24\frac{3}{4}$ kts. **Boilers:** 18. **Fuel:** 2,756 tons coal. **Radius:** 6,500/4,400 mls at 10/14 kts. **Armour:** belt $9\frac{3}{4}$ in, turrets 9 in, deck $2\frac{1}{2}$ in. **Crew:** 923

Conte di Cavour **(I)** **1911**

Gave her name to a class of three battleships, being preceded into service by sister ships *Giulio Cesare* and *Leonardo da Vinci*.

Conte di Cavour was rebuilt at Trieste between 1933–7: her horizontal and underwater protection was greatly improved; more powerful machinery (93,433 hp) was installed and this, combined with a lengthened hull, raised her best speed to 28¾ kts; the midship turret was removed to compensate for increased top-weight; and the remaining ten guns were bored out to 12.6-in to increase their maximum range from 28,900 to 36,000 yards. New superstructures replaced the former upperworks. Displacement rose to 23.622 tons.

Built: Naval Dockyard, Spezia (Aug. '10–Apr. '15). **Dimensions:** 557¾×91¾×28¾ ft = 21,750 tons. **Armament:** 13 12-in (LA), 18 4.7-in (LA), 13 3-in (LA) guns; 3 17.7-in (submerged) TTs. **Machinery:** 4-shaft steam turbines, 31,278 hp = 22¼ kts. **Boilers:** 20. **Fuel:** 1,300 tons coal+930 tons oil. **Radius:** 4,800/2,900 mls at 10/19 kts. **Armour:** belt 9¾ in, turrets 9¾ in, deck 1¾ in. **Crew:** 1,000

Princess Royal (GB) 1911

Second of three Lion class battle-cruisers to enter service in 1912–13 (the last unit – *Queen Mary* – was sunk at Jutland). Known in the vernacular of the Service as the 'Splendid Cats', these were the first British warships to cost over £2 million.

She was one of the four 'contingent dreadnoughts' authorized in 1909, in addition to the four original units of that year's programme, to compensate for the recent increase in German capital ship construction. The doubling of the British programme was a direct result of a hard-fought political campaign with the now famous slogan 'We want eight and we won't wait!'

The primary battery was mounted in four twin turrets – two forward, one amidships (between the second and third funnels), and one aft.

Built: Vickers, Barrow (May '10–Nov. '12). **Dimensions:** $700 \times 88\frac{1}{2} \times 26\frac{1}{2}$ ft = 26,270 tons. **Armament:** 8 13.5-in (LA), 16 4-in (LA) guns; 2 21-in (submerged) TTs. **Machinery:** 4-shaft steam turbines, 78,600 hp = $28\frac{1}{2}$ kts. **Boilers:** 42. **Fuel:** 3,500 tons coal + 1,135 tons oil. **Radius:** 5,610/2,420 mls at 10/24 kts. **Armour:** belt 9 in, turrets 9 in, deck $2\frac{1}{2}$ in. **Crew:** 997

Kongo (J) 1912

By placing the contract for this battle-cruiser with a British shipyard, the Japanese were able to benefit from the expertise of one of the world's leading builders of large warships. So successful was this privately designed ship, that the Admiralty was compelled to redesign the fourth unit of the Lion class, HMS *Tiger*, on similar lines.

Kongo was the prototype for three more ships, *Hiei*, *Haruna* and *Kirishima*, built in Japan for completion in 1914–15. The entire class was twice modernized between the wars, and re-rated as battleships. They were provided with improved horizontal and underwater protection, and fitted with pagoda-type (combined mast and bridge) superstructures, together with effective AA batteries. More powerful machinery was installed, which raised maximum speed to $30\frac{1}{4}$ kts.

Built: Vickers, Barrow (Jan. '11–Aug. '13). **Dimensions:** $704 \times 92 \times 27\frac{1}{2}$ ft = 26,330 tons. **Armament:** 8 14-in (LA), 16 6-in (LA), 16 12-pdr (LA) guns; 8 21-in (submerged) TTs. **Machinery:** 4-shaft steam turbines, 64,000 hp = $27\frac{1}{2}$ kts. **Boilers:** 36. **Fuel:** 4,200 tons coal+1,000 tons oil. **Radius:** 8,000 mls at 14 kts. **Armour:** belt 8 in, turrets 9 in, deck $2\frac{3}{4}$ in. **Crew:** 1,221

30

Warspite (GB) 1913

Second of five Queen Elizabeth class battleships to enter service during 1915–16. These very successful vessels had a 3-knot-speed advantage over their contemporaries, which was achieved by installing more powerful machinery and extra boilers in lieu of a midship turret. For the first time in capital ships, their two-dozen boilers were of the all-oil-burning variety, which further contributed to high speed.

The 15-in battery fired a heavier broadside (15,360 lb) than did ten 13.5-in guns (14,000 lb) in previous super-dreadnoughts. Each 15-in could achieve a range of 23,400 yards with full (20°) elevation. Magazine capacity was 848 projectiles, or 106 rounds per gun.

The entire class (with the exception of the name-ship) constituting the 5th Battle Squadron was at Jutland, where *Warspite* withstood thirteen heavy shell hits. Rebuilt at Portsmouth in 1934–7, she was then flagship of the Mediterranean Fleet

until WWII. She saw more action and enjoyed more success than any other British battleship, although being severely damaged on several occasions. She was sold for scrap in 1946.

The photograph (*left*) depicts HMS *Warspite* in her original appearance soon after commissioning. The second picture (*below*) shows the degree of alteration she underwent during her reconstruction in the mid 1930s.

Sister ships were *Queen Elizabeth, Barham, Valiant* and *Malaya.*

Built: HM Dockyard, Devonport (Oct. '12–Mar. '15). **Dimensions:** $643\frac{3}{4} \times 90\frac{1}{2} \times 30\frac{1}{8}$ ft = 29,150 tons. **Armament:** 8 15-in (LA), 14 6-in (LA) guns; 4 21-in (submerged) TTs. **Machinery:** 4-shaft steam turbines, 75,000 hp = 24 kts. **Boilers:** 24. **Fuel:** 3,400 tons oil. **Radius:** 4,400 mls at 10 kts. **Armour:** belt 13 in, turrets 13 in, deck 3 in. **Crew:** 951

Erin (GB) 1913

Launched in September 1913 as the *Reshadieh*, one of two battleships being fitted out in British yards for the Imperial Ottoman Navy at the outbreak of hostilities in August 1914. Both units were requisitioned by the British Government and incorporated into the Royal Navy. The compulsory acquisition of these ships was so resented by Turkey that this action may well have contributed to her alliance with Germany.

Erin's design was similar to that of contemporary British 'super-dreadnought' battleships, so called because of their 13.5-in armament with its centre-line disposition, which enabled a full ten-gun broadside to be fired on either beam. Fought at Jutland 1916, *Erin* was scrapped in 1923.

Built: Vickers, Barrow (Aug. '11–Aug. '14). **Dimensions:** $559\frac{1}{2} \times 91\frac{1}{2} \times 28\frac{2}{3}$ ft = 22,780 tons. **Armament:** 10 13.5-in (LA), 16 6-in (LA) guns; 4 21-in (submerged) TTs. **Machinery:** 4-shaft steam turbines, 26,500 hp = 21 kts. **Boilers:** 15. **Fuel:** 2,120 tons coal + 710 tons oil. **Radius:** 5,300 mls at 10 kts. **Armour:** belt 12 in, turrets 11 in, deck $1\frac{1}{2}$ in. **Crew:** 1,070

Ark Royal (GB) 1914

Begun as a commercial collier, but taken over by the Admiralty while still on the stocks for conversion to a seaplane carrier, she became the first ship built specially to operate the heavier-than-air flying machine. Eight seaplanes were stowed in the holds, from which they were conveyed by two steam cranes (clearly visible in the photograph) to the water alongside for take-off. On landing, recovery was performed in a similar manner. This process, however, was essentially a calm-water operation. Alternatively, a flying-off deck was provided forward, which enabled aeroplanes and/or seaplanes (aided by a launching trolley) to become airborne when the ship was steaming dead into wind at full speed. Re-named *Pegasus*.

During WWII she served as a fighter catapult ship, providing air cover for convoys, until relegated to an accommodation ship in 1944. Sold for mercantile service in 1947 and re-named *Anita I*.

Built: Blyth Sbdg, Northumberland (Est. '13–Dec. '14). **Dimensions:** $366 \times 50\frac{3}{4} \times 17\frac{1}{2}$ ft = 7,020 tons. **Armament:** 8 seaplanes+2 aeroplanes; 4 12-pdr (AA) guns. **Machinery:** 1-shaft reciprocating (VTE), 3,000 hp = $10\frac{1}{2}$ kts. **Boilers:** 2. **Fuel:** 500 tons oil. **Crew:** 140/180

Baden (D) 1915

Second battleship of the Bayern class to enter service in 1916. Their main battery marked a considerable jump in calibre (an increase of three inches over the previous class), giving the Kaiserliche Marine parity in size of capital-ship ordnance with the RN for the first time.

In March 1917 *Baden* assumed the role of flagship of the C-in-C High Seas Fleet. Interned at Scapa Flow in December 1918. Six months later attempts by her crew to scuttle the ship were thwarted by a British salvage party who managed to beach her. Temporarily repaired and towed to Portsmouth, where a detailed inspection was made of her design, which provided valuable information for future construction. Sunk as a target by British battleships in 1921.

Built: Schichau, Danzig (Sept. '13–Oct. '16). **Dimensions:** $623\frac{1}{3} \times 99 \times 27\frac{3}{4}$ ft = 28,074 tons. **Armament:** 8 15-in (LA), 16 5.9-in (LA), 4 3.4-in (AA) guns; 5 23.6-in (submerged) TTs. **Machinery:** 3-shaft steam turbines, 52,815 hp = $22\frac{1}{4}$ kts. **Boilers:** 14. **Fuel:** 3,346 tons coal + 610 tons oil. **Radius:** 5,000 mls at 12 kts. **Armour:** belt $13\frac{3}{4}$ in, turrets, $13\frac{3}{4}$ in, deck $4\frac{3}{4}$ in. **Crew:** 1,171

Argus (GB) 1917

Laid down as the *Conte Rosso*, a luxury liner ordered by the Italian Lloyd Sabaudo Line. Construction was suspended at the outbreak of war and not resumed until August 1916, when she was purchased by the Admiralty for conversion to an aircraft carrier. Completed with a flush, full-length flight deck, providing for the first time a practical platform on which aeroplanes could land, as well as take off. Hitherto, landing-on decks had been fitted, abaft the superstructure and funnel, on a few ships. But the upperworks and furnace gases collectively created severe air turbulence and eddies, which made landing exceedingly perilous. Sited well forward on each side of the flight deck were two small bridges. Between these was a retractable charthouse. Smoke passed through two horizontal side ducts.

Built: Beardmore, Glasgow (1914–Sept. '18).
Dimensions: 565×68×21 ft = 14,450 tons.
Armament: 20 aircraft (2 lifts); 6 4-in (AA) guns. **Machinery:** 4-shaft steam turbines, 22,000 hp = 20½ kts. **Boilers:** 12. **Fuel:** 2,000 tons oil. **Crew:** 495

Curacoa (GB) 1917

Light cruiser of the C class, of which twenty-eight examples were completed between 1914–22. These were subdivided into six groups: *Curacoa* belonged to the penultimate group, together with *Cardiff*, *Ceres*, *Coventry* and *Curlew*. These ships were designed for operations in the North Sea, and had sufficient speed to enable them either to combine tactically with destroyers in the defence of the fleet, or to act independently as scouts.

Curacoa served in Admiral Tyrwhitt's famous Harwich Force from completion to the Armistice.

Mined in the Baltic in 1919, during the Russian campaign. Converted to an ack-ack ship in 1939. Lost off the Irish coast in October 1942, when accidentally rammed by the liner, *Queen Mary*.

Built: HM Dockyard, Pembroke (July '16–Feb. '18). **Dimensions:** $450 \times 43\frac{1}{2} \times 14\frac{1}{4}$ ft = 4,190 tons. **Armament:** 5 6-in (LA), 2 3-in (AA) guns; 8 21-in (twin) TTs. **Machinery:** 2-shaft steam turbines, 40,000 hp = 29 kts. **Boilers:** 6. **Fuel:** 950 tons oil. **Radius:** 1,625/2,240 mls at 27/24 kts. **Armour:** belt 3 in, shields 1 in, deck 1 in. **Crew:** 327

Eagle (GB) 1918

Had the Great War not occurred, this vessel would have been completed as the Chilean battleship *Almirante Cochrane* in 1916, mounting ten 14-in guns on a displacement of 28,600 tons. However, construction was suspended from the outbreak of hostilities, until the ship was purchased by the Admiralty in July 1917 for conversion to an aircraft carrier.

She was the first carrier to have the now-commonplace island-type superstructure (bridge, funnel, mast, etc.), forming a single streamlined unit on the extreme starboard side), which leaves the flight deck totally unobstructed.

Most of her war career was spent in the Mediterranean, where she was sunk by a U-boat in August 1942 while on Operation Pedestal.

Built: Armstrong Whitworth, Newcastle (Jan. '13–Oct. '23). **Dimensions:** $667\frac{1}{2} \times 105\frac{1}{4}$ (fd: 96) $\times 21\frac{3}{4}$ ft = 22,600 tons. **Armament:** 21 aircraft (2 lifts); 9 6-in (LA), 5 4-in (AA) guns. **Machinery:** 4-shaft steam turbines, 50,000 hp = 24 kts. **Boilers:** 32. **Fuel:** 3,750 tons oil. **Armour:** belt 7 in, deck $1\frac{1}{2}$ in. **Crew:** 748

Hood (GB) 1918

One of four battle-cruisers ordered in 1916 to counter similar ships under construction in German yards. As none of the latter ever reached fruition, sister ships *Anson*, *Howe* and *Rodney* were cancelled; only *Hood* was sufficiently advanced to warrant completion.

In 1917 an additional 5,000 tons of armour were worked into *Hood*'s design, which brought her more into the fast battleship category. Until the completion of the *Bismarck* in 1940, she was the largest and fastest capital ship in the world. Major reconstruction was to have started in 1939, but was prevented by the outbreak of WWII. This left *Hood* with totally inadequate deck armour.

As Vice-Admiral Holland's flagship in May 1941, she intercepted the *Bismarck* in the Denmark Strait, where she was sunk by the German ship.

Built: John Brown, Clydebank (Sept. '16–Mar. '20). **Dimensions:** $860\frac{1}{2} \times 105\frac{1}{4} \times 28\frac{1}{2}$ ft = 41,200 tons. **Armament:** 8 15-in (LA), 12 5.5-in (LA), 4 4-in (AA) guns; 6 21-in (2 submerged) TTs. **Machinery:** 4-shaft steam turbines, 144,000 hp = 31 kts. **Boilers:** 24. **Fuel:** 4,000 tons oil. **Radius:** 6,300 mls at 12 kts. **Armour:** belt 12 in, turrets 15 in, deck 3 in. **Crew:** 1,477

Luce (USA) 1918

One of the famous and highly successful flush-deck destroyers that were mass-produced after America's entry into WWI. Affectionately termed the 'four stackers', they totalled 273 units, subdivided into three groups: six prototypes, the Wickes class (111) to which *Luce* belonged, and the Clemson class (156). As contemporaries of the British V & W class, it is interesting to draw comparisons between the two types. Although lacking an all-centreline disposition of the main armament (the 4-in guns being arranged fore and aft, and one a side amidships) they mounted an exceedingly powerful torpedo armament.

It was announced in September 1940 that fifty of the remaining flush-deckers were to be transferred to the RN, in exchange for 99-year leases on bases in Newfoundland and the West Indies.

Built: Fore River Sbdg, Massachusetts (Feb. '18–Sept. '18). **Dimensions:** $314\frac{1}{3} \times 31 \times 9$ ft = 1,154 tons. **Armament:** 4 4-in (LA), 1 3-in (AA) guns; 12 21-in (triple) TTs. **Machinery:** 2-shaft steam turbines, 26,000 hp = 35 kts. **Boilers:** 4. **Radius:** 4,300 mls at 14 kts. **Crew:** 102

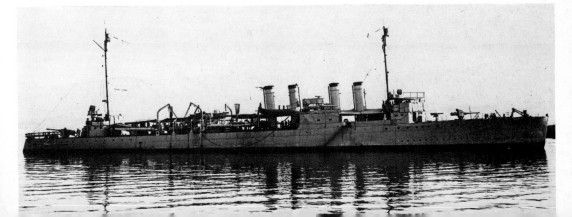

Westminster (GB) 1918

Representative of the V & W class that introduced the superfiring arrangement of the main armament to destroyer design, i.e. four guns in single mountings (4.7-in in later ships) carried on the centreline, two forward and two aft, with the inner pair superimposed over the other two. Sixty-seven units of the class were completed either during, or shortly after the war, while thirty-eight more were cancelled after the Armistice. An excellent design, this set the pattern for British and foreign construction in this category for the next twenty years.

After WW1 *Westminster* and three of her sisters were the first destroyers to be equipped with the new AS detection device, Asdic.

Built: Scotts' Sbdg, Greenock (Apr. '17–Apr. '18). **Dimensions:** $312 \times 29\frac{1}{2} \times 10\frac{2}{3}$ ft = 1,316 tons. **Armament:** 4 4-in (LA), 1 3-in (AA) guns; 6 21-in (triple) TTs. **Machinery:** 2-shaft steam turbines, 27,000 hp = 34 kts. **Boilers:** 3. **Fuel:** 367 tons oil. **Radius:** 3,500/900 mls at 15/32 kts. **Crew:** 110

Hermes (GB) 1919

First aircraft carrier to be designed and built as such from the keel up. With the signing of the Armistice in November 1918 all incentive was lost to rush this vessel into service, thus allowing the Japanese *Hosho* (7,470 tons) the distinction of becoming the world's first custom-built carrier to enter service early in 1923, although laid down three months after the British ship was launched.

Hermes was moved from her builders to Devonport in 1920 for completion. She proved a fine seaboat, and in spite of her moderate size, carried as many aircraft as some earlier but larger carrier conversions. However, with the installation of a second lift (and a catapult), and the increase in size of naval aircraft, by 1939 hangar capacity had been reduced to about a dozen machines.

Sunk by IJN dive-bombers off the coast of Ceylon in April 1942.

Built: Armstrong Whitworth, Newcastle (Jan. '18–Feb. '24). **Dimensions:** $598 \times 70\frac{1}{4}$ (fd: 90) $\times$ $18\frac{3}{4}$ ft = 10,850 tons. **Armament:** 20 aircraft (1 lift); 6 5.5-in (LA), 3 4-in (AA) guns. **Machinery:** 2-shaft steam turbines, 40,000 hp = 25 kts. **Boilers:** 6. **Fuel:** 2,000 tons oil. **Armour:** belt 3 in, deck 1 in. **Crew:** 664

Nagato (J) 1919

First ship of Japan's ambitious '8-8 Plan' that called for the construction of an equal number of battleships and battle-cruisers, of which the largest would have mounted 18-in guns on a displacement of 47,500 tons. All sixteen vessels were scheduled for completion by 1927. However, only two were completed as capital ships and two more as aircraft carriers, while the remainder were cancelled under the terms of the Washington Treaty of 1922.

Nagato was the only one of Japan's twelve battleships to survive the war, and was surrendered in 1945. She sank when used by the Americans as a target during the A-bomb tests conducted at Bikini atoll in July 1946.

Her sister ship, *Mutsu*, was accidentally lost in June 1943 from an internal explosion.

Built: Naval Dockyard, Kure (Aug. '17–Nov. '20). **Dimensions:** $708 \times 95 \times 29\frac{3}{4}$ ft = 32,720 tons. **Armament:** 8 16-in (LA), 20 5.5-in (LA), 4 3-in (AA) guns; 8 21-in (4 submerged) TTs. **Machinery:** 4-shaft steam turbines, 80,000 hp = $26\frac{3}{4}$ kts. **Boilers:** 21. **Fuel:** 1,600 tons coal + 3,400 tons oil. **Radius:** 5,500 mls at 16 kts. **Armour:** belt 12 in, turrets 14 in, deck $2\frac{1}{2}$ in. **Crew:** 1,333

Akagi (J) 1925

Begun as a battle-cruiser of the Amagi class, of which four units were to have been completed in 1923–4, to mount ten 16-in guns on a displacement of 40,000 tons. Construction was arrested in February 1922 under the terms of the Washington Treaty, but resumed in November 1923 for conversion to an aircraft carrier. As completed, she had three flight decks, so that aircraft could take off from the two lower units forward and land on the uppermost deck. No bridge structure was provided, while the two funnels protruded from just below the main flight deck on the starboard side.

In August 1938 she emerged from a major refit (as shown). The two lower flying-off decks were dispensed with in favour of extra hangar space, to increase capacity to ninety-one aircraft.

Akagi was the flagship of the six-carrier task force whose aircraft attacked Pearl Harbor in December 1941. Still flying the flag of Vice-Admiral Nagumo in June 1942, she was sunk by USN aircraft at the Battle of Midway.

Built: Naval Dockyard, Kure (Dec. '20–Mar. '27). **Dimensions:** $855\frac{1}{3} \times 95$ (fd:100) $\times 26\frac{1}{2}$ ft = 26,900 tons. **Armament:** 60 aircraft (2 lifts); 10 7.9-in (LA), 12 4.7-in (AA) guns. **Machinery:** 4-shaft steam turbines, 131,000 hp = $32\frac{1}{2}$ kts. **Boilers:** 19. **Fuel:** 2,100 tons coal+3,900 tons oil. **Radius:** 8,200 mls at 16 kts. **Armour:** belt 10 in. **Crew:** 2,000

Lexington (USA) 1925

Originally gave her name to a class of six battle-cruisers (to have displaced 43,500 tons, and mounted eight 16-in guns) whose construction was abandoned as a result of the Washington Naval Treaty of 1922. However, Treaty rules permitted two of these, *Lexington* and *Saratoga*, to be completed as aircraft carriers. Four sister ships, *Constellation*, *Constitution*, *Ranger* and *United States*, were dismantled on their slipways. As carriers, they were not exceeded in size or speed until WWII. A distinctive feature was the enormous 79-ft funnel sited on the starboard side abaft the bridge structure. The 8-in guns were mounted in twin turrets, two before and two abaft the island.

Lexington was severely damaged by IJN aircraft during the Battle of the Coral Sea in May 1942, and had to be sunk by a friendly destroyer.

Built: Bethlehem Steel Co, Massachusetts (Jan. '21–Dec. '27). **Dimensions:** 888×105½ (fd: 130)×24¼ ft = 33,000 tons. **Armament:** 90 aircraft (1 catapult and 2 lifts); 8 8-in (LA), 12 5-in (AA) guns. **Machinery:** 4-shaft turbo-electric drive, 180,000 hp = 33¼ kts. **Boilers:** 16. **Fuel:** 8,884 tons oil. **Armour:** belt 6 in, hangar deck 3 in, turrets 3 in. **Crew:** 2,122

Nelson (GB) 1925

One of two concessionary battleships whose construction was permitted during the Washington Treaty's ten-year 'building holiday' to compensate Britain for the 16-in gunned units of the American Maryland and Japanese Nagato (qv) classes.

Nelson's design, and that of her sister *Rodney*, was a telescoped version of four 48,000-ton battle-cruisers ordered in 1921, but cancelled in compliance with Treaty rules. All nine 16-in guns were grouped forward of the bridge in triple turrets. This arrangement minimized the length of the citadel that enclosed the ship's vitals, and allowed a concentration of armour over this area.

Nelson was mined in December 1939, which put her out of action for eight months, but she performed valuable service for the rest of WWII.

Built: Armstrong Whitworth, Newcastle (Dec. '22–June '27). **Dimensions:** 710×106×28½ ft = 33,950 tons. **Armament:** 9 16-in (LA), 12 6-in (HA), 6 4.7-in (AA), 8 2-pdr (AA) guns; 2 24.5-in (submerged) TTs. **Machinery:** 2-shaft steam turbines, 45,000 hp = 23 kts. **Boilers:** 8. **Fuel:** 4,000 tons oil. **Radius:** 16,500/5,500 mls at 12/23 kts. **Armour:** belt 14 in, turrets 16 in, deck 6¼ in. **Crew:** 1,314

Amazon (GB) 1926

In 1918 Britain had a superabundance of destroyers well in excess of her peace-time requirements, the majority of which were soon scrapped. It was more than five years before the Admiralty invited the country's five shipbuilders who specialized in destroyer construction to submit designs for a new standard type of vessel. This was to be based on the V & W class (page 40), but incorporating post-war developments.

The designs submitted by Thornycroft and Yarrow were accepted, contracts were placed in 1924 with each company for a single prototype, to be evaluated against one another for their respective merits. Yarrow built the *Ambuscade*. Both prototypes served as AS escorts during WWII, and were broken up shortly after the cessation of hostilities.

Built: Thornycroft, Southampton (Jan. '25–Sept. '26). **Dimensions:** 323×31½×9½ ft = 1,352 tons. **Armament:** 4 4.7-in (LA), 2 2-pdr (AA) guns; 6 21-in (triple) TTs. **Machinery:** 2-shaft steam turbines, 39,500 hp = 37 kts. **Boilers:** 3. **Fuel:** 433 tons oil. **Radius:** 3,400 mls at 15 kts. **Crew:** 138

Cumberland (GB) 1926

First and longest serving of Britain's famous County class cruisers. Thirteen were completed during 1928–30, including two for the RAN. They were designed to take full advantage of the upper limits imposed by the Washington Treaty for cruiser construction.

Dubbed 'tinclads' due to the absence of side armour, although a 5-in belt was retrofitted in some units. Protection was augmented by compartmentation and external bulges.

The high endurance of the County class made them ideal for patrolling Britain's Empire trade routes. Refitted 1935–6 and converted to a trials ship in 1949, *Cumberland* was scrapped in 1959.

Built: Vickers, Barrow (Oct. '24–Jan. '28). **Dimensions:** $630 \times 68\frac{1}{3} \times 16\frac{1}{4}$ ft = 10,000 tons. **Armament:** 8 8-in (HA), 4 4-in (AA), 4 2-pdr (AA) guns; 8 21-in (quadruple) TTs. **Machinery:** 4-shaft steam turbines, 80,000 hp = $31\frac{1}{2}$ kts. **Boilers:** 8. **Fuel:** 3,400 tons oil. **Radius:** 10,400/2,300 mls at economical and full speed respectively. **Armour:** turrets 2 in, deck 4 in. **Crew:** 679

Ashigara (J) 1928

Last of four heavy cruisers belonging to the Nachi class to be commissioned into the IJN during 1928–9. They mounted the largest calibre of gun permitted under the terms of the Washington Treaty, but exceeded the tonnage limitation by nearly 10 per cent.

The main battery was disposed in twin turrets, three forward and two aft. During her 1934–6 refit the single 4.7-in guns were replaced by four twin 5-in mountings, and bulges increased her beam to 68 ft. Again refitted 1939–40, additional TTs were mounted, and the AA armament was augmented. By this time displacement had risen to 13,380 tons, reducing speed to $33\frac{3}{4}$ knots.

During WWII this class constituted the Fifth Cruiser Division, in which *Ashigara* became one of Japan's most celebrated warships. Torpedoed and sunk by HM submarine *Trenchant* in 1945.

Built: Kawasaki, Kobe (Apr. '25–Aug. '29).
Dimensions: $661\frac{3}{4} \times 56\frac{3}{4} \times 19\frac{1}{3}$ ft = 10,940 tons.
Armament: 10 8-in (LA), 6 4.7-in (AA) guns; 12 24-in (triple) TTs; 2 aircraft (1 catapult).
Machinery: 4-shaft steam turbines, 130,000 hp = $35\frac{1}{2}$ kts. **Boilers:** 12. **Fuel:** 2,000 tons oil.
Radius: 8,000 mls at 14 kts. **Armour:** belt 4 in, turrets 3 in, deck 3 in. **Crew:** 773

Glorious (GB) 1930

First commissioned in 1917 as a light battle-cruiser with a main armament consisting of four 15-in guns in twin turrets. Conversion to an aircraft carrier was started at Rosyth, but on the closure of that yard she was towed to Devonport.

Her flight deck measured 590×100 ft, below which were two hangars, one on top of the other, with a combined capacity for forty-eight aeroplanes. Immediately forward of the upper hangar was a flying-off deck for fighters. She had one of the finest AA batteries mounted in any ship up to that time.

In June 1940 *Glorious* was homeward bound from the Norwegian campaign, laden with RAF fighters, when she was intercepted and sunk by the battle-cruisers *Scharnhorst* and *Gneisenau*.

Sister carrier, *Courageous*, was sunk by a U-boat two weeks after the declaration of WWII.

Converted: HM Dockyard, Rosyth (Feb. '24–Jan. '30). **Dimensions:** $786\frac{1}{4}$×$90\frac{1}{2}$(fd: 100) × 24 ft = 22,500 tons. **Armament:** 48 aircraft (2 catapults and 2 lifts); 16 4.7-in (AA) guns. **Machinery:** 4-shaft steam turbines, 90,000 hp = $30\frac{1}{2}$ kts. **Boilers:** 18. **Fuel:** 3,940 tons oil. **Armour:** belt 3 in, lower deck 3 in. **Crew** 1,216

Achilles (GB) 1932

Second of five Leander class cruisers to be completed for the RN between 1933–5, she was followed into service by *Orion*, *Ajax* and *Neptune*. The design was the first prepared by a signatory power to depart from both of the Washington Treaty's upper limits of 10,000 tons and 8-in guns for this category of ship, and as such was more in accordance with the RN's requirement for a cruiser of moderate proportions.

While on loan to the RNZN in December 1939, *Achilles*, in company with *Ajax* and the heavy cruiser *Exeter*, defeated the *Admiral Graf Spee* during the Battle of the River Plate.

Achilles was transferred to the Indian Navy in July 1948, and renamed *Delhi*.

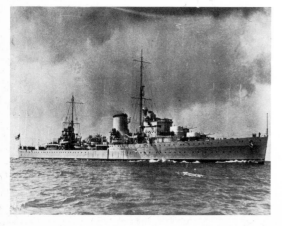

Built: Cammel Laird, Birkenhead (June '31– Oct. '33). **Dimensions:** $554\frac{1}{2} \times 55\frac{1}{4} \times 16$ ft = 7,030 tons. **Armament:** 8 6-in (HA), 4 4-in (AA), 12 0.5-in (AA) guns; 8 21-in (quadruple) TTs; 1 aircraft (1 catapult). **Machinery:** 4-shaft steam turbines, 72,000 hp = 32 kts. **Boilers:** 4. **Fuel:** 1,800 tons oil. **Radius:** 12,000 mls at economical speed. **Armour:** belt 4 in, turrets 1 in, deck 2 in. **Crew:** 550

Ranger (USA) 1933

The USN's first purpose-built aircraft carrier. Hangars were not incorporated within the hull, as in the Lexington class, but built on top of it, forming part of a huge superstructure, which added nothing to structural strength. This set a trend for American carrier design for the next twenty years. An island was provided on the starboard beam, but smoke and gases were discharged through six hinged funnels which could be lowered during flying operations, three on each side of the flight deck. *Ranger*'s moderate dimensions reflected the USN's desire to spread the remaining 69,000 tons allocated to it for carrier construction under the terms of the Washington Treaty into five small units. However, as she was too small, slow and ill-protected for front-line duties, her design was not repeated.

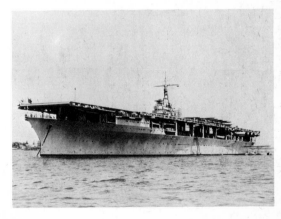

Built: Newport News, Virginia (Sept. '31–June '34). **Dimensions:** 769×80(fd: 109½)×19¾ ft = 14,500 tons. **Armament:** 86 aircraft (1 catapult and 2 lifts); 8 5-in (AA) guns. **Machinery:** 2-shaft steam turbines, 53,500 hp = 29½ kts. **Boilers:** 6. **Fuel:** 3,207 tons oil. **Armour:** belt 2 in, deck 1 in. **Crew:** 1,788

Le Terrible (F) 1933

Destroyer of the six-unit Le Fantasque class, which also comprised *L'Audacieux*, *L'Indomptable*, *Le Malin* and *Le Triomphant*.

The design typifies the French practice of building large and costly destroyers, rated as *contre torpilleurs*, during the inter-war years. The armament carried in these ships was comparable to that mounted in some contemporary light cruisers.

While on sea trials, *Le Terrible* established a new world speed record for a destroyer (which still stands) slightly in excess of 45 knots. She maintained this speed for an hour, developing about 100,000-shaft horse-power.

She saw service with the Allies during the latter part of WWII. Decommissioned in 1957, *Le Terrible* was used as a static training ship until being broken up in 1962.

Built: Ch. Navales Francais, Blainville (Nov. '31–Oct. '35). **Dimensions:** $434\frac{1}{3} \times 40\frac{1}{2} \times 14$ ft = 2,569 tons. **Armament:** 5 5.5-in (LA), 4 37-mm (AA), 4 13-mm (AA) guns; 9 21.7-in (triple) TTs. **Machinery:** 2-shaft steam turbines, 74,000 hp = 37 kts. **Boilers:** 4. **Fuel:** 580 tons oil. **Radius:** 2,500 mls at 24 kts. **Crew:** 210.

Admiral Graf Spee   (D)   1934

The Versailles Peace Treaty of June 1919 relegated the German Navy from the world's second most powerful to a token force suitable only for coastal defence. This was spearheaded by six obsolete pre-dreadnought battleships, which could be replaced only on reaching twenty years of age by vessels displacing not more than 10,000 tons. These materialized in the form of three revolutionary units. Dubbed 'pocket battleships', although officially rated as *panzerschiffe* (armoured ships), they were designed as commerce raiders, which could outshoot any cruiser and outrun most battleships. Despite the use of several weight-saving techniques in construction, displacement still exceeded the Treaty limit by 21 per cent. Diesel propulsion produced unprecedented endurance for this size of vessel, which attained speeds of up to 28½ knots on trials.

Built: Naval Dockyard, Wilhelmshaven (Oct. '32– Jan. '36). **Dimensions:** 616¾×71¾×19 ft = 12,100 tons. **Armament:** 6 11-in (LA), 8 5.9-in (LA), 6 4.1-in (AA), 8 37-mm (AA), 10 20-mm (AA) guns; 8 21-in (quadruple) TTs; 2 seaplanes (1 catapult). **Machinery:** 2-shaft diesel engines, 56,000 hp = 26 kts. **Fuel:** 2,756 tons oil. **Radius:** 19,000/8,900 mls at 10/20 kts. **Armour:** belt 4 in, turrets 5 in, deck 3 in. **Crew:** 1,124

Dunkerque (F) 1935

With sister ship *Strasbourg*, she was built to counter the trio of German 'pocket battleships' described on page 53. Their design was inspired by the British Nelson class, with the entire main armament carried before the bridge in quadruple turrets. To localize the effects of shell hits, the two main turrets were staggered, and internally subdivided by armoured bulkheads to separate each pair of guns into individual compartments. The 13-in guns could each fire up to three 1,258-lb shells per minute to a maximum range of 45,800 yards. A trainable catapult was sited on the quarterdeck, forward of which was a hangar for four Loire-Nieuport 130 seaplanes.

Both ships were scuttled at Toulon in November 1942 to prevent their falling into Axis hands.

Built: Naval Dockyard, Brest (Dec. '32–Apr. '37). **Dimensions:** $703\frac{3}{4} \times 102\frac{1}{4} \times 28\frac{3}{4}$ ft = 26,500 tons. **Armament:** 8 13-in (LA), 16 5.1-in (DP), 8 37-mm (AA), 32 13-mm (AA) guns; 4 seaplanes (1 catapult). **Machinery:** 4-shaft steam turbines, 112,500 hp = $29\frac{1}{2}$ kts. **Boilers:** 6. **Fuel:** 6,500 tons oil. **Radius:** 7,500 mls at 15 kts. **Armour:** belt $9\frac{3}{4}$ in, turrets 13 in, deck 5 in. **Crew:** 1,381

Sheffield (GB) 1936

Light cruiser of the Southampton class, whose eight units were completed between 1937–9. These very successful ships were the first British cruisers to be built with hangars, positioned one a side (each housing a Walrus amphibian) abreast the fore funnel, forming a continuation aft of the bridge structure. An athwartship catapult was placed between the funnels for launching, while two adjacent cranes were provided for recovery purposes.

Each 6-in gun fired up to eight 112-lb shells per minute to a maximum range of 24,800 yards.

Of this class, *Southampton*, *Manchester* and *Gloucester* became war losses; *Birmingham*, *Newcastle*, *Glasgow* and *Liverpool* were scrapped, 1958–60; *Sheffield* was broken up in 1967.

Built: Vickers-Armstrongs, Newcastle (Jan. '35– Aug. '37). **Dimensions:** $591\frac{1}{2} \times 61\frac{2}{3} \times 17$ ft = 9,100 tons. **Armament:** 12 6-in (LA), 8 4-in (AA), 8 2-pdr (AA), 8 0.5-in (AA) guns; 6 21-in (triple) TTs; 2 aircraft (1 catapult). **Machinery:** 4-shaft steam turbines, 75,000 hp = 32 kts. **Boilers:** 4. **Fuel:** 1,970 tons oil. **Radius:** 7,000 mls at 14 kts. **Armour:** belt $4\frac{1}{2}$ in, turrets 2 in, deck 2 in. **Crew:** 700

Ark Royal (GB) 1937

The culmination of some twenty years' development in carrier design during the inter-war period, *Ark Royal* became the prototype for all future British fleet aircraft carriers. A double-storeyed hangar, covering almost the entire length of the ship, was designed to accommodate up to seventy-two aircraft, though sixty proved more feasible.

During the first two years of WWII, *Ark Royal* was often 'sunk' by German propaganda. On one such occasion, the pilot of a Junkers 88 received the Iron Cross. These claims were made by William Joyce ('Lord Haw-Haw') in his radio broadcasts.

It was a torpedo from one of the *Ark Royal*'s Swordfish that disabled the *Bismarck*. On several occasions *Ark Royal* ferried RAF fighters to Malta. Returning from one such mission in November 1941 she was sunk by a U-boat.

Built: Cammell Laird, Birkenhead (June '35–Dec. '38). **Dimensions:** 800 × 94¾ (fd: 96) × 22¾ ft = 22,000 tons. **Armament:** 60 aircraft (2 catapults and 3 lifts); 16 4.5-in (DP), 48 2-pdr (AA), 32 0.5-in (AA) guns. **Machinery:** 3-shaft steam turbines, 102,000 hp = 30¾ kts. **Boilers:** 6. **Fuel:** 4,620 tons oil. **Armour:** belt 4½ in, hangar deck 3 in. **Crew:** 1,575

Cossack (GB) 1937

One of the sixteen Tribal class destroyers which were completed for the RN in 1938–9. These were built to counter the large and heavily armed destroyers that were then either in service or under construction for foreign navies.

The emphasis of the Tribal design was placed on a main armament of eight 4.7-in guns (mounted in pairs, two forward and two aft) which had 40° elevation, and fired 50-lb shells.

Cossack achieved international fame in February 1940 when she entered the neutral waters of the Norwegian Jösenfjord, and members of her crew boarded the German naval auxiliary *Altmark* to liberate 299 British prisoners, all of whom were survivors from the merchant ships sunk by the *Admiral Graf Spee* the previous year. *Cossack* was sunk by a U-boat in October 1941.

Built: Vickers-Armstrongs, Newcastle (June '36–June '38). **Dimensions:** $377 \times 36\frac{1}{2} \times 9$ ft = 1,959 tons. **Armament:** 8 4.7-in (LA), 4 2-pdr (AA), 8 0.5-in (AA) guns; 4 21-in (quadruple) TTs; 20 DCs for 2 stern rails. **Machinery:** 2-shaft steam turbines, 44,000 hp = 36 kts. **Boilers:** 3. **Fuel:** 524 tons oil. **Radius:** 5,700/3,200 mls at 15/20 kts. **Crew:** 219

Craven (USA) 1937

Destroyer of the Gridley class, of which twenty-two units were completed between 1938–40. Five of these became war losses.

As completed, the Gridley class mounted numerically the most powerful torpedo armament ever borne by a destroyer, which was disposed in four quadruple (two a side) banks of TTs. On a qualitative basis, however, Japanese destroyers had the edge over their American counterparts, as they were armed with the 24-in oxygen-driven 'Long Lance' torpedo. This was fitted with a 1,100-lb warhead, and had a range of 43,500 yards at 36 knots.

Craven was scrapped in 1947, together with most of the other survivors of her class. Seven of her sister ships were used as targets during the atomic tests at Bikini atoll in July 1946.

Built: Bethlehem Steel Co., Massachusetts (June '35–July '38). **Dimensions:** $341\frac{2}{3} \times 34\frac{2}{3} \times 9\frac{3}{4}$ ft = 1,500 tons. **Armament:** 4 5-in (DP), 4 1.1-in (AA) guns; 16 21-in (quadruple) TTs; plus AS weapons. **Machinery:** 2-shaft steam turbines, 42,800 hp = $36\frac{1}{2}$ kts. **Boilers:** 4. **Fuel:** 600 tons oil. **Radius:** 6,000 mls at 15 kts. **Crew:** 172

Vittorio Veneto (I) 1937

First battleship of the Littorio class to enter service with the Italian Navy. Two sister ships, *Italia* (ex-*Littorio*) and *Roma*, were commissioned in May 1940 and June 1942 respectively. A fourth unit of the class, the uncompleted *Impero*, was broken up soon after the war.

Under the terms of Italy's armistice her fleet was placed under Allied control at Malta. *Vittorio Veneto* was surrendered there in September 1943. After the war she was returned to Italy, but paid off in February 1948, and scrapped at La Spezia over the next two years.

Built: Cantieri Riuniti dell' Adriatico, Trieste (Oct. '34–Apr. '40). **Dimensions:** $774\frac{1}{4} \times 108 \times 31\frac{1}{2}$ ft = 41,167 tons. **Armament:** 9 15-in (LA), 12 6-in (LA), 12 3.5-in (AA), 20 37-mm (AA), 20 20-mm (AA) guns; 3 seaplanes (1 catapult). **Machinery:** 4-shaft steam turbines, 134,616 hp = $31\frac{1}{2}$ kts. **Boilers:** 8. **Fuel:** 4,000 tons oil. **Radius:** 4,580 mls at 16 kts. **Armour:** belt $13\frac{3}{4}$ in, turrets $11\frac{3}{4}$ in, deck $6\frac{1}{3}$ in. **Crew:** 1,600

Belfast (GB) 1938

Improved Southampton class cruiser, seen here while running contractor's sea trials, before the secondary armament, fire control apparatus, TTs, etc., had been installed. Armour protection over the ship's vitals was designed to resist 8-in shell-fire, whilst internal subdivision was excellent.

In November 1939 *Belfast* broke her back on detonating a magnetic mine, which put her out of action for three years. During the ensuing refit, bulges were fitted, increasing her beam by $5\frac{2}{3}$ feet. For the remainder of WWII, and again during the Korean War she gave yeoman service. She under-

went a £$5\frac{1}{2}$ million refit at Devonport in 1956–9. Now a museum ship near Tower Bridge.

Only sister ship, *Edinburgh*, was sunk by German naval forces in May 1942.

Built: Harland & Wolff, Belfast (Dec. '36–Aug. '39). **Dimensions:** $613\frac{1}{2} \times 63\frac{1}{3} \times 17\frac{1}{4}$ ft = 10,000 tons. **Armament:** 12 6-in (LA), 12 4-in (AA), 16 2-pdr (AA), 8 0.5-in (AA) guns; 6 21-in (triple) TTs; 2 aircraft (1 catapult). **Machinery:** 4-shaft steam turbines, 80,000 hp = 32 kts. **Boilers:** 4. **Fuel:** 2,260 tons oil. **Radius:** 8,000 mls at 14 kts. **Armour:** belt $4\frac{1}{2}$ in, turrets $2\frac{1}{2}$ in, deck 3 in. **Crew:** 850

Jupiter (GB) 1938

One of a class of eight destroyers completed in 1939, which introduced longitudinal framing to British destroyer construction. Other units of the J class were *Jackal, Jaguar, Janus, Jersey, Juno, Javelin* and *Jervis.*

Up to 250 shells were provided for each 4.7-in gun. A quadruple 2-pdr pom-pom was mounted immediately abaft the funnel, while two sets of multiple 0.5-in machine-guns were carried in the bridge wings. The quintuple banks of TTs were mounted on the centreline abaft the funnel,

although early in the war a single 4-in AA gun was shipped in lieu of the after set of tubes.

Jupiter was torpedoed and sunk by Japanese destroyers during the Battle of Java Sea in 1942.

Built: Yarrow, Glasgow (Sept. '37–June '39). **Dimensions:** $356\frac{1}{2} \times 35\frac{2}{3} \times 9$ ft = 1,760 tons. **Armament:** 6 4.7-in (LA), 4 2-pdr (AA), 8 0.5-in (AA) guns; 10 21-in (quintuple) TTs; 20 DCs for 2 DCTs and 1 stern rail. **Machinery:** 2-shaft steam turbines, 40,000 hp = 36 kts. **Boilers:** 2. **Fuel:** 484 tons oil. **Radius:** 5,500/3,700 mls at 15/20 kts. **Crew:** 183

St Louis (USA) 1938

Penultimate unit of nine Brooklyn class cruisers to enter service during 1937–9. These were built to counter the Japanese Mogami class cruisers, which mounted a comparable main armament in five similarly disposed triple turrets, i.e. three forward and two aft. *St Louis'* main battery fired 102¼-lb projectiles to a maximum range of 26,000 yards, with a rate of fire of ten rounds a minute.

The hangar, situated in the after section of the hull, accounted for the high freeboard and transom stern, and accommodated up to six seaplanes, together with spare parts and maintenance facilities. Hangar and after-decks were connected by a single lift, while catapults were sited on either quarter, with a crane placed between them at the stern. Sold to Brazil in 1951, and re-named *Tamandaré*.

Built: Newport News, Virginia (Dec. '36–Dec. '39). **Dimensions:** 608½×61¾×19¾ ft = 10,000 tons. **Armament:** 15 6-in (LA), 8 5-in (DP), 8 0.5-in (AA) guns; 4 seaplanes (2 catapults and 1 lift). **Machinery:** 4-shaft steam turbines, 100,000 hp = 34 kts. **Boilers:** 8. **Fuel:** 2,200 tons oil. **Radius:** 7,600 mls at 15 kts. **Armour:** belt 5 in, turrets 5 in, deck 3 in. **Crew:** 888

Bismarck (D) 1939

First battleship built in Germany since WWI, and only sister ship to the *Tirpitz*. Construction of both vessels was legalized by the Anglo-German Naval Treaty of June 1935.

Bismarck's armour protection accounted for about 40 per cent of her displacement, while internally she was a veritable honeycomb of water-tight compartments.

In May 1941 *Bismarck* with the heavy cruiser, *Prinz Eugen*, sailed from Gdynia in a bid to break into the Atlantic to attack Allied convoys. *En route* she sank the *Hood*, but received three 14-in hits from the *Prince of Wales*. She was then torpedoed by an FAA Swordfish. Completely crippled by gunfire from British battleships, she was scuttled by her crew, of whom only 115 survived.

Built: Blohm & Voss, Hamburg (July '36–Aug. '40). **Dimensions:** $822\frac{3}{4} \times 118\frac{1}{4} \times 28\frac{1}{2}$ ft = 41,700 tons. **Armament:** 8 15-in (LA), 12 5.9-in (LA), 16 4.1-in (AA), 16 37-mm (AA), 12 20-mm (AA) guns; 6 seaplanes (1 athwartship catapult). **Machinery:** 3-shaft steam turbines, 150,170 hp = 30 kts. **Boilers:** 12. **Fuel:** 7,800 tons oil. **Radius:** 8,100 mls at 19 kts. **Armour:** belt $12\frac{1}{2}$ in, turrets 14 in, deck 8 in. **Crew:** 2,092

King George V (GB) 1939

Gave her name to a class of five battleships. The main armament and displacement of these ships were limited (to 14-in and 35,000 tons respectively) by the second London Naval Treaty of 1936, although the first stipulation was never ratified.

The 14-in guns were disposed in quadruple turrets fore and aft, and a superimposed twin turret before the bridge structure.

In May 1941 *K.G.V.* played a major role in the destruction of the *Bismarck*. Post-war she served with the Home Fleet until being laid up in a state of preservation (cocooned) as part of the Reserve Fleet. She was broken up in 1958.

Sister ships, *Prince of Wales, Duke of York, Anson* and *Howe*, completed in 1941–2.

Built: Vickers-Armstrongs, Newcastle (Jan. '37–Dec. '40). **Dimensions:** 745×103×29 ft = 36,750 tons. **Armament:** 10 14-in (LA), 16 5.25-in (DP), 32 2-pdr (AA), 16 0.5-in (AA) guns; 4 seaplanes (1 athwartship catapult). **Machinery:** 4-shaft steam turbines, 110,000 hp = 29 kts. **Boilers:** 8. **Fuel:** 3,842 tons oil. **Radius:** 15,000/6,300/3,200 mls at 10/20/27 kts. **Armour:** belt 15 in, turrets 13 in, deck 6 in. **Crew:** 1,640

Shokaku (J) 1939

With sister ship *Zuikaku*, generally considered the most successful of all Japanese aircraft carriers. Designed to operate the monoplanes then under development, notably the famous Zero fighter, they were provided with a small island on the starboard side, abaft which were two funnels projecting from below the flight deck. Machinery was the most powerful ever installed in a Japanese warship.

On commissioning, they formed the Fifth Carrier Division of the First Air Fleet. Both took part in the attack on Pearl Harbor, the timing of which was influenced by their availability. Later, either one or both took part in virtually every carrier operation of the Pacific War, with the notable exception of the Midway action. *Shokaku* was sunk by the American submarine *Cavalla* during the Battle of the Philippine Sea in 1944. *Zuikaku* was lost during the Battle of Leyte Gulf.

Built: Naval Dockyard, Yokosuka (Dec. '37–Aug. '41). **Dimensions:** $844\frac{3}{4} \times 85\frac{1}{3} \times 29$ ft = 25,675 tons. **Armament:** 84 aircraft (2 catapults and 3 lifts); 16 5-in (AA), 36 25-mm (AA) guns. **Machinery:** 4-shaft steam turbines, 160,000 hp = $34\frac{1}{4}$ kts. **Boilers:** 8. **Fuel:** 5,000 tons oil. **Radius:** 9,700 mls at 18 kts. **Armour:** belt $8\frac{1}{2}$ in, hangar deck $6\frac{3}{4}$ in. **Crew:** 1,660

Hornet (USA) 1940

Last aircraft carrier to be completed for the USN before America's entry into WWII. Two sister ships, *Yorktown* and *Enterprise*, were commissioned in 1937 and 1938 respectively.

In April 1942 *Hornet* launched sixteen Army B-25 bombers for the first air raids against the Japanese home islands, one of the targets being Tokyo. At the Battle of Midway in June 1942 aircraft from *Hornet* and her two sisters sank four Japanese carriers, *Akagi*, *Kaga*, *Soryu* and *Hiryu*, all of which had participated in the attack on Pearl Harbor six months earlier. The loss of these ships, together with some 250 combat aircraft, marked the reversal of fortunes in the Pacific. *Yorktown* was also lost during this action. In October *Hornet* was sunk on the Santa Cruz Islands campaign. *Enterprise* was scrapped 1958.

Built: Newport News, Virginia (Sept. '39–Oct. '41). **Dimensions:** $827 \times 83\frac{1}{4}$ (fd: 114) $\times 21\frac{3}{4}$ ft = 19,900 tons. **Armament:** 80+ aircraft (2 catapults and 3 lifts); 8 5-in (DP), 16 1.1-in (AA), 16 0.5-in (AA) guns. **Machinery:** 4-shaft steam turbines, 120,000 hp = 33 kts. **Boilers:** 9. **Fuel:** 6,400 tons oil. **Radius:** 12,700 mls at 15 kts. **Armour:** belt 4 in, hangar deck 3 in. **Crew:** 1,889

Indomitable (GB) 1940

One of six vessels which formed the backbone of Britain's carrier fleet during WWII. Three sister ships, *Illustrious*, *Formidable* and *Victorious*, entered service during 1940–1; two improved units, *Indefatigable* and *Implacable*, were completed in 1944.

A novel aspect of their design was the armoured flight deck (forming the hangar roof), built to withstand 1,000-lb AP bombs released from less than 4,500 feet.

While under construction, *Indomitable*'s design was modified to incorporate a lower 'half' hangar aft for an extra squadron of aircraft. Later in the war deck-parking and outriggers further increased her capacity to sixty-five aircraft.

Built: Vickers-Armstrongs, Barrow (Nov. '37–Aug. '41). **Dimensions:** $754 \times 95\frac{3}{4} \times 25$ ft = 23,500 tons. **Armament:** 48 aircraft (1 catapult and 2 lifts); 16 4.5-in (DP), 48 2-pdr (AA), 8 20-mm (AA) guns. **Machinery:** 3-shaft steam turbines, 111,000 hp = $30\frac{1}{2}$ kts. **Boilers:** 6. **Fuel:** 4,850 tons oil. **Radius:** 10,000 mls at 15 kts. **Armour:** belt $4\frac{1}{2}$ in, hangar sides $1\frac{1}{2}$ in, flight deck 3 in. **Crew:** 1,392

Yamato (J) 1940

The *Yamato* and sister ship *Musashi* were the largest and most powerful battleships ever built. Two further units of the class, *Shinano* and *No. 111*, were laid down in 1940; the former was completed as an aircraft carrier, while the latter was dismantled on the slipway, owing to shortages.

The main armament was mounted in three triple turrets, two forward and one aft. Each 18.1-in gun (the largest ever carried afloat) fired 3,220-lb shells to a range of 45,275 yards with full (45°) elevation. During the course of the war, the AA battery was constantly being augmented, reaching its zenith in 1945 when it comprised twenty-four 5-in and 146 25-mm guns. Massive armour protection accounted for about $33\frac{1}{3}$ per cent of displacement. The belt was impervious to 18-in shells fired from 22,000 yards or more, and the deck armour was designed to withstand a 2,200-lb bomb released from 10,000 feet or less. This was backed up by a total of 1,147 watertight compartments built within the hull (of which all but eighty-two were below the armoured deck).

The decision to build these leviathans was based on the Japanese realization that they could not hope to compete with the United States in terms of capital ships on a quantitative basis, in view of the latter's vastly superior industrial capacity. Nevertheless, they considered that the US advantage could be counteracted by building battleships on a qualitative basis.

The top photograph depicts *Yamato* running trials. The second picture shows her during the Battle of Leyte Gulf in October 1944.

In 1945 *Yamato* fitted out as a 'Kamikaze' with sufficient fuel to take her to Okinawa, where she was to operate offshore as a floating fortress, harassing American amphibious invasion forces. Having exhausted her supply of ammunition, she would have been run aground, with her crew joining the army in the defence of the island. However, before reaching her destination she was sunk by US carrier-borne aircraft.

Built: Naval Dockyard, Kure (Nov. '37–Dec. '41).
Dimensions: $863 \times 127\frac{3}{4} \times 35\frac{1}{2}$ ft = 64,170 tons.
Armament: 9 18.1-in (LA), 12 6.1-in (HA), 12 5-in (AA), 24 25-mm (AA) guns; 6 seaplanes (2 catapults and 1 lift). **Machinery:** 4-shaft steam turbines, 150,000 hp = 27 kts. **Boilers:** 12.
Fuel: 6,300 tons oil. **Radius:** 7,200 mls at 27 kts.
Armour: belt 16 in, turrets $25\frac{1}{2}$ in, deck $7\frac{3}{4}$ in.
Crew: 3,332

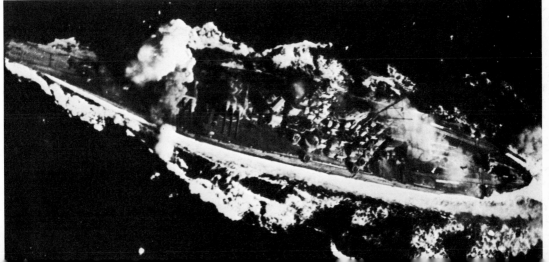

Juneau (USA) 1941

Anti-aircraft cruiser of the Atlanta class, of which eleven examples were completed during 1942–6. The primary role of these ships was to provide air defence for fast carrier task forces. Their design, which may well have been influenced by the contemporary British Dido class, was a complete breakaway from American cruiser development.

The main battery of sixteen semi-automatic 5-in guns was mounted in twin turrets, six on the centreline disposed equally forward and aft, and one on each side abreast the after superstructure. Each barrel could sustain a rate of fire of fifteen rounds per minute, discharging 54-lb shells to a maximum range of 18,200 yards, or to a ceiling of 37,200 feet with full (85°) elevation.

Juneau was sunk by a Japanese submarine during the Guadalcanal campaign in 1942.

Built: Federal Sbdg, New Jersey (May 1940–2).
Dimensions: $541\frac{1}{2} \times 53\frac{1}{4} \times 16\frac{1}{2}$ ft = 6,000 tons.
Armament: 16 5-in (DP), 12 1.1-in (AA) guns; 8 21-in (quadruple) TTs. **Machinery:** 2-shaft steam turbines, 75,000 hp = 33 kts. **Boilers:** 4.
Fuel: 1,450 tons oil. **Radius:** 7,500 mls at 15 kts.
Armour: belt $3\frac{1}{2}$ in, turrets $1\frac{1}{2}$ in, deck 2 in.
Crew: 600.

Long Island (USA) 1941

Launched in January 1940 as the merchantman SS *Mormacmail*, she was converted into the USN's first escort aircraft carrier. This type of vessel, which could be produced cheaply and quickly by using standard merchant hulls, was urgently required to provide air cover for convoys in areas of ocean beyond the range of land-based aircraft. A further 123 escort carriers were either built or converted in American yards between 1941–5, thirty-nine of which were transferred to the RN under Lend-Lease. These proved particularly successful in containing U-boat operations during the Battle of the Atlantic, by combining with small AS escorts to form 'hunter–killer' groups.

Long Island's wooden flight deck originally measured 362×102 ft (as shown), but after trials this was lengthened to 439 ft, and a catapult was installed at its fore end. Unlike succeeding classes, no island was provided.

Converted: Newport News, Virginia (Mar. '41–June '41). **Dimensions:** 492×69½(fd: 102)×25¾ ft = 7,886 tons. **Armament:** 21 aircraft (1 lift); 1 5-in (DP), 2 3-in (AA), 10 20-mm (AA) guns. **Machinery:** 1-shaft diesel engines, 8,500 hp = 17½ kts. **Fuel:** 1,429 tons oil. **Crew:** 950

Essex (USA) 1942

Gave her name to a class of twenty-four fleet aircraft carriers which were completed between 1942–50. Eight further units were cancelled in 1945. Fourteen received their baptism of fire in WWII, during which their presence in the Pacific made American domination in that theatre of the war absolute. Members of the class have also seen action in both the Korean and Vietnam wars.

An outboard elevator was carried — in addition to the two centreline lifts — on the port side opposite the island. This could be raised (as shown above right) to the vertical position, to allow passage through the Panama Canal.

Eight 5-in guns were mounted in twin turrets (two at each end of the island superstructure), while the remainder were arranged in single mountings along the port side of the flight deck.

These proved extremely tough ships, capable of absorbing considerable battle damage and surviving, a fact cruelly put to the test by Japanese Kamikaze attacks during the latter part of the war.

Although up to 107 aircraft could originally be accommodated, albeit by close stowage, maximum capacity was eventually reduced to about forty, due to the increased size of combat aircraft.

Essex was extensively modernized during the 1950s, along with fourteen of her sisters, when she received an enclosed 'hurricane' bow, angled deck, etc. She was relegated from the attack status to an ASW role in March 1960. Decommissioned in June 1969 and placed in reserve after a total of twenty-two years' active service, she was deleted from the Navy List in June 1973.

The top photograph depicts USS *Essex* soon after completion, with an axial flight deck, while the second picture shows her as rebuilt in the mid '50s with an angled deck.

Built: Newport News, Virginia (Apr. '41–Dec. '42). **Dimensions:** 872×93(fd: 147½)×23 ft = 27,100 tons. **Armament:** 85+ aircraft (2 catapults and 3 lifts); 12 5-in (DP), 68 40-mm (AA), 52 20-mm (AA) guns. **Machinery:** 4-shaft steam turbines, 150,000 hp = 33 kts. **Boilers:** 8. **Fuel:** 6,161 tons oil. **Armour:** belt 3 in, hangar deck 3 in. **Crew:** 3,500

Spartan (GB) 1942

Improved Dido class cruiser, of which five examples were completed between 1943–4. These were easily distinguishable from the eleven units of the first group (commissioned 1940–2), which had heavily raked funnels and masts and a third turret before the bridge.

Hull and machinery were similar to the pre-war Arethusa class cruiser, while mounting a 5.25-in armament in twin turrets. This semi-automatic weapon fired 82-lb shells, at a rate of fire of ten rounds per gun per minute up to a range of 22,500 yards, or a ceiling of about 40,000 feet.

Served with the Home Fleet, until being transferred to the Mediterranean, where she was sunk by German aircraft during the Anzio landings in January 1944. *Spartan's* sisterships were *Bellona*, *Black Prince*, *Diadem* and *Royalist*.

Built: Vickers-Armstrongs, Barrow (1939–43).
Dimensions: 512×50½×15 ft = 5,900 tons.
Armament: 8 5.25-in (DP), 12 2-pdr (AA), 12 20-mm (AA) guns; 6 21-in (triple) TTs. **Machinery:** 4-shaft steam turbines, 62,000 hp = 32½ kts. **Boilers:** 4. **Fuel:** 1,100 tons oil. **Radius:** 4,240/3,480/1,500 mls at 16/20/30 kts. **Armour:** belt 3 in, turrets 2 in, deck 2 in. **Crew:** 550

Buckley (USA) 1943

Gave her name to the second of six classes of destroyer escort to be put into mass-production in American yards during WWII. The initial order for this category of ship was placed on behalf of the RN in mid-1941, to meet British specifications for operations in the North Atlantic. A total of 565 destroyer escorts was built, of which seventy-eight were transferred to the RN under Lend-Lease. These vessels proved particularly successful against submarines, when operating with an escort carrier as a hunter—killer group. At the same time they performed their intended role of protecting convoys splendidly.

Buckley was the first destroyer escort to be built to USN requirements for service in the Pacific. She was deleted from the Navy List in June 1968.

Built: Bethlehem Steel Co., Massachusetts (1942–3). **Dimensions:** $306 \times 36\frac{3}{4} \times 9\frac{1}{4}$ ft = 1,400 tons. **Armament:** 3 3-in (DP), 2 40-mm (AA), 10 20-mm (AA) guns; 3 21-in (triple) TTs; 1 Hedgehog DCM, 8 DCTs and 2 stern rails. **Machinery:** 2-shaft turbo-electric drive, 12,000 hp = 24 kts. **Boilers:** 2. **Fuel:** 340 tons oil. **Radius:** 5,000 mls at 15 kts. **Crew:** 220

Caprice (GB) 1943

Representative of the standard type of fleet destroyer put into mass-production under the Emergency War Programme. In all 112 units were completed between 1941–7, which were sub-divided into fourteen flotillas, each of eight vessels.

Caprice underwent a mid-life refit by her builders in 1959 (as shown), when her AS capabilities were enhanced by the substitution of two Squid 3-barrelled DCMs in lieu of her after superimposed 4.5-in gun and original AS armament. The bridge was enclosed, and the after bank of TTs was replaced by a deckhouse for extra accommodation. Later the forward set of tubes was also suppressed to compensate for extra top-weight created by the installation of a Seacat SAM system.

Built: Yarrow, Glasgow (Sept. '42–Apr. '44). **Dimensions:** $362\frac{3}{4} \times 35\frac{2}{3} \times 10$ ft = 1,710 tons. **Armament:** 4 4.5-in (DP), 2 40-mm (AA), 6 20-mm (AA) guns; 8 21-in (quadruple) TTs; 70 DCs for 4 DCTs and 2 stern rails. **Machinery:** 2-shaft steam turbines, 40,000 hp = $36\frac{3}{4}$ kts. **Boilers:** 2. **Fuel:** 580 tons oil. **Radius:** 1,300 mls at 32 kts. **Crew:** 186

McCord (USA) 1943

A destroyer of the highly successful Fletcher class, of which no fewer than 175 examples were commissioned during 1942–5. The largest group of fleet destroyers to be built to a single design during WWII, they became the mainstay of the USN's Pacific Fleet in this category.

The five semi-automatic 5-in guns were housed in single turrets, two forward and three aft. Of the close-range AA battery, the 40-mm Bofors were carried in pairs, while the 20-mm Oerlikons were distributed in single mountings. Quintuple banks of TTs were sited abaft each funnel. The 21-in torpedoes launched from these had a maximum range of 4,500 yards at 46 knots.

After the war the Fletchers saw extensive service: many were transferred to foreign navies, and are still going strong.

Built: Bethlehem, San Francisco (Mar. '42–Aug. '43). **Dimensions:** $376\frac{1}{2} \times 39\frac{1}{3} \times 12\frac{1}{4}$ ft = 2,050 tons. **Armament:** 5 5-in (DP), 6 40-mm (AA), 10 20-mm (AA) guns; 10 21-in (quintuple) TTs; 6 DCTs and 2 stern rails. **Machinery:** 2-shaft steam turbines, 60,000 hp = 37 kts. **Boilers:** 4. **Fuel:** 650 tons oil. **Radius:** 6,000 mls at 15 kts. **Crew:** 300

De Ruyter (N) 1944

One of a pair of light cruisers ordered shortly before the outbreak of WWII. Spasmodic construction continued during the occupation of Holland, and she was launched by the Germans in December 1944 as the *De Zeven Provincien* (but later exchanged names with her sister). Work was resumed by the Dutch to a revised design.

The main armament is carried on the centreline in four twin turrets, conventionally arranged, two forward and two aft. Each 6-in gun can fire up to fifteen shells per minute, and achieve a maximum 60° elevation at which aircraft can be engaged.

The 57-mm battery is mounted in double turrets: two in superfiring positions over the main armament fore and aft, and the remainder winged out amidships. Both primary and secondary batteries are radar-controlled, while the 40-mm guns are visually directed.

Sold to Peru in 1972 as the *Almirante Grau*.

Built: Wilton-Fijenoord, Schiedam (Sept. '39–Nov. '53). **Dimensions:** $614\frac{1}{2} \times 56\frac{3}{4} \times 18\frac{1}{2}$ ft = 9,529 tons. **Armament:** 8 6-in (HA), 8 57-mm (AA), 8 40-mm (AA) guns. **Machinery:** 2-shaft steam turbines, 85,000 hp = 32 kts. **Boilers:** 4. **Armour:** belt 3 in, turrets 4 in. **Crew:** 926

Magnificent (GB) 1944

One of sixteen light fleet aircraft carriers launched between 1943–5. Divided into two groups, the first ten were of the Colossus class which completed in 1944–6, while the remainder belonged to the Majestic class: *Magnificent* was the first.

To achieve rapid construction, their design excluded armour protection and had a simplified hull arrangement with modest internal subdivision, and, wherever possible, existing equipment was installed. To minimize top-weight, the built-in aerial defence was limited to a battery of light AA guns. Up to the hangar deck, the hull was built to Lloyd's specifications, enabling these vessels to be easily converted for post-war mercantile service. However, since they were highly economical to operate with an ability to handle modern piston-engined aircraft, all were retained for peace-time naval duties.

Built: Harland & Wolff, Belfast (July '43–May '48). **Dimensions:** $698 \times 80\frac{1}{4}$ (fd: $112\frac{1}{2}$) × 21 ft = 15,700 tons. **Armament:** 34 aircraft (1 catapult and 2 lifts); 30 40-mm (AA) guns. **Machinery:** 2-shaft steam turbines, 40,000 hp = $24\frac{1}{2}$ kts. **Boilers:** 4. **Fuel:** 3,200 tons oil. **Radius:** 12,000/6,200 mls at 14/23 kts. **Crew:** 1,100

Missouri (USA) 1944

Last of four Iowa class battleships to be commissioned into the USN between 1943–4 she was preceded into service by *Iowa*, *New Jersey* and *Wisconsin*. Two uncompleted sister ships – *Illinois* and *Kentucky* – were broken up after the war. The Iowas were the fastest battleships ever built and, except for the Japanese Yamato class, were also the largest. These were the last battleships to be built in American yards. Their 16-in guns fired 2,700-lb shells to a maximum range of twenty-three miles.

Missouri served in the Pacific during WWII, providing close-range AA cover for fast carrier task forces, and bombarding invasion objectives in support of amphibious assault operations. As flagship of the US 3rd Fleet, the document of unconditional surrender was signed by the Japanese aboard *Missouri* on 2 September 1945, while she was lying at anchor in Tokyo Bay.

Subsequently employed as a training ship, she was the USN's only active battleship between 1948–50, and served in the fire support role during the Korean War of 1950–3. Decommissioned 1955, and placed in reserve at Bremerton, Washington, she is still in existence at the time of writing.

Built: New York N.Yd, New Jersey (Jan. '41–June '44). **Dimensions:** $887\frac{1}{4} \times 108\frac{1}{4} \times 29$ ft = 48,500 tons. **Armament:** 9 16-in (LA), 20 5-in (DP), 80 40-mm (AA), 49 20-mm (AA) guns; 3 aircraft (2 catapults). **Machinery:** 4-shaft steam turbines, 212,000 hp = 35 kts. **Boilers:** 8. **Fuel:** 7,251 tons oil. **Radius:** 15,000 mls at 12 kts. **Armour:** belt 12 in, turrets 17 in, deck 6 in. **Crew:** 1,921

Modeste (GB) 1944

One of twenty-five escort sloops belonging to the modified Black Swan class to be completed during 1942–6, including two for the RIN. Five more were cancelled in 1945. Of the British vessels, three became war losses, while others included *Amethyst*, of River Yangtze fame, and *Starling*, which sank fourteen U-boats.

Developed from a pre-war design, the class was capable of performing both AS and AA duties. Their modest speed was no handicap in their AS role, as Asdic was unusable at speeds in excess of

20 kts; while for AA duties they were fitted with Denny-Brown stabilizers that made them steady gun platforms for aerial defence. Excellent sea-boats, they were employed mainly in the protection of convoys in the North Atlantic.

Built: HM Dockyard, Chatham (Feb. '43–Sept. '45) **Dimensions:** $299\frac{1}{2} \times 38\frac{1}{2} \times 9$ ft = 1,490 tons. **Armament:** 6 4-in (AA), 8 40-mm (AA) guns; 1 Hedgehog DCM, 110 DCs for 4 DCTs and 2 stern rails. **Machinery:** 2-shaft steam turbines, 4,300 hp = $19\frac{3}{4}$ kts. **Boilers:** 2. **Fuel:** 370 tons oil. **Radius:** 4,500 mls at 12 kts. **Crew:** 192

Vanguard (GB) 1944

Largest British warship ever built, and the RN's final battleship. Ordered under the War Construction Programme in 1940. Evolved from the King George V class, her design benefited from those ships' operational experience.

The pronounced sheer and flare in the forward section of the hull, aided by a trio of breakwaters on the forecastle, kept 'A' and 'B' turrets relatively dry when at speed or in adverse weather conditions. On completion her 15-in guns were thirty years old, being the ordnance formerly mounted in the light battle-cruisers *Glorious* and *Courageous*.

The turrets and mountings were modified prior to installation, raising full elevation to 30° for a maximum range of 32,000 yards. In addition she had the most devastating AA battery ever borne by a British capital ship. She was scrapped 1960.

Built: John Brown, Clydebank (Oct. '41–Apr. '46). **Dimensions:** $814\frac{1}{3} \times 108 \times 31$ ft = 44,500 tons. **Armament:** 8 15-in (LA), 16 5.25-in (DP), 71 40-mm (AA) guns. **Machinery:** 4-shaft steam turbines, 130,000 hp = $29\frac{1}{2}$ kts. **Boilers:** 8. **Fuel:** 4,868 tons oil. **Radius:** 9,000 mls at 20 kts. **Armour:** belt 14 in, turrets 13 in, deck 6 in. **Crew:** 1,600

Bulwark (GB) 1948

Basically an expansion of the Majestic class (page 79), but with more powerful machinery.

Conversion to a commando ship (the RN's equivalent to the USN's amphibious assault ship described on page 103) at Portsmouth Dockyard in 1959–60 involved the removal of catapults, arrester wires and eight 40-mm guns. Internally the ship was made habitable for 600 troops (later 900), and facilities provided for the maintenance and operation of up to twenty large transport helicopters. Vehicles and other heavy equipment are stowed on the after part of the flight deck, while four landing craft are suspended from davits, two on each side, aft of amidships.

Three sister ships, *Centaur*, *Albion* and *Hermes*, were completed in 1953, 1954 and 1959.

Built: Harland & Wolff, Belfast (May '45–Nov. '54). **Dimensions:** $737\frac{3}{4} \times 90$ (fd: $123\frac{1}{2}$) ×23 ft = 22,000 tons. **Armament:** 45 aircraft (2 catapults and 2 lifts); 26 40-mm (AA) guns. **Machinery:** 2-shaft steam turbines, 76,000 hp = $29\frac{1}{2}$ kts. **Boilers:** 4. **Fuel:** 4,200 tons oil. **Armour:** flight deck 1 in. **Crew:** 1,330

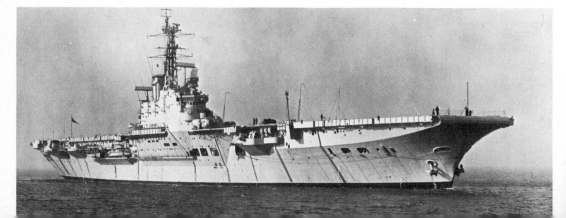

Ark Royal (GB) 1950

One of four large fleet aircraft carriers ordered in 1942 under the Emergency War Programme. These were named *Audacious*, *Irresistible*, *Africa* and *Eagle*, but the last pair was cancelled in 1945, while the first two were renamed *Eagle* and *Ark Royal* respectively. These became the largest carriers ever built for the RN.

Ark Royal's design incorporated most of the improvements that had been derived from war experience, with particular emphasis being paid to underwater and hangar protection. Her con-struction was intermittent, and she remained on the slipway for a full seven years. This delay, however, allowed several post-war features to be worked into her design, including an 'interim' ($5\frac{1}{2}°$) angled deck, steam catapults (in place of the hydraulic variety) and an outboard elevator (removed 1959).

She underwent a £$32\frac{1}{2}$ million refit at Devonport in 1967–70, which enables her to operate F-4K Phantom interceptors. Alterations included in-creasing the angle of the flight deck to $8\frac{1}{2}°$, installing more powerful steam catapults, enlarging the island superstructure, and providing new

air-surveillance radar. As modernized, no built-in armament is shipped, although provision was made for the eventual installation of four Seacat SAM systems.

On the flight deck, (shown left, as modernized), are Mach 2 Phantom interceptors, transonic Buccaneer strike aircraft and Gannet AEW (Airborne Early Warning) aircraft, with a Buccaneer loaded on the waist catapult ready for launching. *Ark Royal* also carries Wessex and Sea King ASW helicopters. 36 aircraft are now carried.

Ark Royal is now the RN's only operational fixed-wing carrier, and will continue in service until being relieved by the first of the new 'through-deck cruisers', HMS *Invincible*, in the late 1970s or early 1980s.

Built: Cammell Laird, Birkenhead (May '43–Feb. '55). **Dimensions:** $808\frac{1}{4} \times 112\frac{3}{4}$ (fd: 158) $\times 33\frac{1}{4}$ ft = 43,340 tons. **Armament:** 80 aircraft (2 catapults and 3 lifts); 16 4.5-in (DP), 40 40-mm (AA) guns. **Machinery:** 4-shaft steam turbines, 152,000 hp = $31\frac{1}{2}$ kts. **Boilers:** 8. **Fuel:** 5,500 tons oil. **Armour:** belt $4\frac{1}{2}$ in, hangar sides $1\frac{1}{2}$ in, flight deck 4 in. **Crew:** 2,345

Duchess (GB) 1951

Duchess and her seven sister ships of the Daring class were the final and largest conventional destroyers to be built for the RN. These highly versatile ships could by virtue of their size perform cruiser reconnaissance duties.

The semi-automatic 4.5-in armament was radar-controlled, and disposed in twin turrets, two forward and one aft. Each gun was provided with 300 rounds of ammunition, and fired up to twenty 55-lb shells per minute, to an accurate range in excess of ten miles. For close-range AA defence, six 40-mm Bofors were arranged in twin mountings, two in the bridge wings and one abaft the second funnel (the fore-funnel was enclosed within the lattice foremast).

Duchess was loaned to the RAN in 1964. She was purchased outright in 1972, and converted to a training ship two years later.

Built: Thornycroft, Southampton (July '48–Oct. '52). **Dimensions:** 390×43×12¾ ft = 2,800 tons. **Armament:** 6 4.5-in (DP), 6 40-mm (AA) guns; 10 21-in (quintuple) TTs; 1 triple Squid DCM. **Machinery:** 2-shaft steam turbines, 54,000 hp = 34¾ kts. **Boilers:** 2. **Fuel:** 584 tons oil. **Radius:** 3,000 mls at 20 kts. **Crew:** 297

Ordzhonikidze (USSR) 1951

Cruiser of the Sverdlov class, a type intended to form the spearhead of Russia's post-war ocean-going fleet. Although rated amongst the most powerful conventional cruisers ever built, they were constructed at a time when this category of warship was becoming obsolete.

A programme originally calling for twenty-four units of this class was initiated by Stalin; but his successor, Nikita Khrushchev, reduced the total to fourteen, scrapping several uncompleted ships.

During a courtesy visit to Portsmouth in April 1956, a British frogman, Commander 'Buster' Crabb, mysteriously disappeared while ostensibly testing underwater equipment. The Russians, however, insisted that he had been examining the hull of this cruiser.

Ordzhonikidze, transferred to the Indonesian Navy in 1962 and re-named *Irian*, was paid off for scrapping in 1972.

Built: Baltiski Yard, Leningrad (1950–3). **Dimensions:** 689×72¼×16 ft = 15,450 tons. **Armament:** 12 6-in (LA), 12 3.9-in (DP), 32 37-mm (AA) guns; 10 21-in (quintuple) TTs; up to 150 mines. **Machinery:** 2-shaft steam turbines, 130,000 hp = 34 kts. **Boilers:** 6. **Fuel:** 3,800 tons oil. **Radius:** 8,700 mls at 18 kts. **Armour:** belt 5 in, turrets 5 in, deck 3 in. **Crew:** 1,050

Hermes (GB) 1953

Although commissioned only five years after her
near-sister ship *Bulwark* entered service, she
incorporated many new features: a 6½° angled
deck; steam catapults; a pair of mirror landing
aids; an outboard elevator on the port side; and
the highly sophisticated Type 984 3-D air-
surveillance radar. For operating in areas con-
taminated by nuclear, biological or chemical
warfare, she is provided with a pre-wetting system
(for washing down her exterior), together with
an air-tight citadel from where the machinery can
be remotely controlled.

Converted to a commando ship between 1971–3
(£25+ million), but with the run-down of
Britain's amphibious warfare squadron *Hermes*
will be further modernized so that her primary
role will become that of ASW.

Built: Vickers-Armstrongs, Barrow (June '44–
Nov. '59). **Dimensions:** 744¼×90 (fd: 144½) ×24
ft = 23,000 tons. **Armament:** 22 aircraft+8
helicopters (2 catapults and 2 lifts); 10 40-mm
(AA) guns. **Machinery:** 2-shaft steam turbines,
76,000 hp = 28 kts. **Boilers:** 4. **Fuel:** 3,880 tons
oil. **Armour:** flight deck 1 in. **Crew:** 1,834

Holland (N) 1953

First destroyer to be designed and built in the Netherlands after WWII. Three sister ships, *Zeeland*, *Noord Brabant*, and *Gelderland*, were completed in 1955. Intended primarily for an AS role, she is equipped with a pair of four-barrelled 375-mm rocket projectors, sited before the bridge abreast 'B' position.

The four 4.7-in guns are radar-controlled, and mounted in fully automatic twin turrets fore and aft. Maximum elevation is 85° (as in 'A' turret below), at which their $51\frac{3}{4}$-lb shells can achieve a vertical range of 40,000 feet, while sustaining a rate of fire of forty rounds per minute. Maximum horizontal range is about 22,000 yards. A single 40-mm AA gun is mounted between the funnels. Unlike their foreign contemporaries, the Hollands were never fitted with torpedo tubes. The class is currently being phased out of service in favour of new construction.

Built: Rotterdamse Droogdok Mij, Rotterdam (Apr. '50–Dec. '54). **Dimensions:** $371 \times 37\frac{1}{2} \times 12\frac{1}{2}$ ft = 2,215 tons. **Armament:** 4 4.7-in (DP) 1 40-mm (AA) guns; 8 375-mm (AS) rocket launchers. **Machinery:** 2-shaft steam turbines, 45,000 hp = 32 kts. **Boilers:** 4. **Crew:** 247

Forrestal (USA) 1954

First of a group of eight gigantic 'super carriers' to be completed for the USN over a period of thirteen years, she was followed into service by the *Saratoga, Ranger* and *Independence* (1956–9), which are essentially similar in design. The last four, *Kitty Hawk, Constellation, America* and *John F. Kennedy* (1961–8) have an improved elevator arrangement, which necessitates the island superstructure being sited farther aft.

The first aircraft carrier to be built to a design of post-war origin, *Forrestal* incorporates all three British inventions to facilitate the operation of jet-propelled aircraft. These are a fully angled flight deck (10½° off the centreline), four steam catapults (each capable of launching two aircraft per minute) and the mirror landing aid. In addition she carries four deck-edge lifts. *Forrestal*'s 5-in guns had all been removed by 1968, and she now has two BPDMSs for close-range air defence.

Built: Newport News, Virginia (July '52–Oct. '55). **Dimensions:** 1,039×129½ (fd: 252)×37 ft = 59,650 tons. **Armament:** 85 aircraft (4 catapults and 4 lifts); 8 5-in (DP) guns. **Machinery:** 4-shaft steam turbines, 260,000 hp = 33 kts.

Boilers: 8. **Fuel:** 7,828 tons oil. **Armour:** belt 5 in, flight deck 5 in. **Crew:** up to 5,000

Boston (USA) 1955

First commissioned in 1943 as a heavy cruiser of the Baltimore class, of which fourteen examples were completed between 1943–6. As converted, she was the world's first operational warship to be armed with supersonic guided missiles.

The installation of the two Terrier systems necessitated the removal of the after triple 8-in turret, and an adjacent twin 5-in mounting. Each launcher had a rate of fire of four rounds per minute, and was served by a rotating magazine with a capacity for 72 missiles.

Employed principally as an escort, she provided air defence for fast carrier groups. However, due to the retention of her forward 8-in battery, she performed valuable service during the Vietnam War in the fire support role (as shown).

Converted: New York Sbdg, New Jersey (Dec. '51–Nov. '55). **Dimensions:** $673\frac{1}{2} \times 70\frac{3}{4} \times 20\frac{1}{2}$ ft = 13,300 tons. **Armament:** 2 twin Terrier SAM launchers; 6 8-in (LA), 10 5-in (DP), 12 3-in (AA) guns. **Machinery:** 4-shaft steam turbines, 120,000 hp = 33 kts. **Boilers:** 4. **Fuel:** 2,500 tons oil. **Radius:** 9,000 mls at 15 kts. **Armour:** belt 6 in, turrets 6 in, deck 3 in. **Crew:** 1,273

Canopo (I) 1955

Centauro class frigate, designed primarily for AA and AS escort duties. Three sister ships, *Castore*, *Centauro* and *Cigno*, were completed in 1957.

The original main armament of four 3-in guns (as shown), was carried in twin turrets fore and aft. These had their guns mounted vertically, one superimposed over the other. This novel disposition enabled both barrels to be served by a single ammunition hoist, which kept weights down to a minimum. Operationally, however, the arrangement proved unsatisfactory, and between 1966–73, both turrets in all four ships were replaced by three single 3-in guns which have a similar rate of fire of about sixty rounds per minute. The extra 3-in mounting (carried aft) also necessitated the removal of the entire 40-mm battery. *Canopo* was so refitted in 1968–9. A 3-barrelled, sonar controlled DCM is mounted in a turret immediately before the bridge. This weapon can fire 12-in DCs to a range well in excess of 1,500 yards.

Built: Cantieri Navali di Taranto (May '52–Apr. '58). **Dimensions:** $338\frac{1}{3} \times 39\frac{1}{2} \times 12\frac{2}{3}$ ft = 1,807 tons. **Armament:** 4 3-in (AA), 4 40-mm (AA) guns; 1 triple DCM, 5 DCTs; 2 21-in (single) TTs.

Machinery: 2-shaft steam turbines, 22,000 hp = 25 kts. **Boilers:** 2. **Fuel:** 400 tons oil. **Radius:** 3,660 mls at 20 kts. **Crew:** 225

Bonaventure (C) 1957

Launched in February 1945 as HMS *Powerful*, one of six light fleet aircraft carriers of the Majestic class. Construction was suspended in May 1946, but resumed to a modified design in July 1952, enabling her to operate jet-propelled aircraft after being bought by the Canadian Government.

Bonaventure's primary role was that of AS warfare, equipped with Tracker (S-2F) AS aircraft and ASW helicopters, although she had a limited strike capability up to 1962, when her squadron of Banshee (F-2H) jet fighters was retired in favour of additional Trackers. Decommissioned in April 1970, she was scrapped in 1971.

Of her five sister carriers, *Terrible* and *Majestic* were sold to Australia, *Hercules* was purchased by India, and *Magnificent* and the uncompleted *Leviathan* were broken up in 1965 and 1968.

Built: Harland & Wolff, Belfast (Nov. '43–Jan. '57). **Dimensions:** $704\frac{3}{4} \times 80\frac{1}{4}$ (fd: 128) $\times 21$ ft = 16,000 tons. **Armament:** 21 aircraft (1 catapult and 2 lifts); 8 3-in (AA) guns. **Machinery:** 2-shaft steam turbines, 40,000 hp = $24\frac{1}{2}$ kts. **Boilers:** 4. **Fuel:** 3,200 tons oil. **Radius:** 12,000/6,200 mls at 14/23 kts. **Crew:** 1,370

Clemenceau (F) 1957

Followed into service two years later by sister ship, *Foch*, these were the first custom-built aircraft carriers to be constructed in France.

Although of comparatively small size, their design embodies all the post-war inventions for the operation of jet-propelled aircraft, namely: an 8° angled flight deck; two mirror landing aids; and two steam catapults, each capable of launching aircraft weighing up to eleven tons. Two $52\frac{1}{2} \times 36$ ft lifts (one on the centreline just forward of the bridge; the second, of the deck-edge variety, immediately abaft the island) connect the flight deck to a single $590\frac{1}{2} \times 78\frac{3}{4} \times 23$ ft hangar. Three flights of aircraft are normally embarked, one each of Crusader interceptors, Etendard IV fighter-bombers, and Breguet Alizé AS machines.

Since completion *Clemenceau*'s beam has been increased by 6 feet, with the fitting of bulges.

Built: Naval Dockyard, Brest (Nov. '55–Nov. '61). **Dimensions:** $869\frac{1}{2} \times 98$ (fd: 168) $\times 24\frac{1}{2}$ ft = 22,000 tons. **Armament:** 40 aircraft (2 catapults and 2 lifts); 8 3.9-in (DP) guns. **Machinery:** 2-shaft steam turbines, 126,000 hp = 32 kts. **Boilers:** 6. **Fuel:** 3,720 tons oil. **Radius:** 7,500/4,800/3,500 mls at 18/24/32 kts. **Crew:** 2,239

Duncan (GB) 1957

Last of twelve second-rate AS frigates of the Blackwood class (Type 14, utility design) to enter service with the RN during 1955–8. Three further units were subsequently delivered to the Indian Navy. All British vessels of this type are named after captains who served under Lord Nelson.

Although only half the displacement and cost of the contemporary Type 12 frigates (page 98), they mount a comparable AS armament to the larger ships. The Limbo DCMs are aimed and fired automatically by sonar, discharging triple salvoes of 400-lb depth bombs, which can then travel over 1,000 yards before entering the water to explode at a predetermined depth around the target.

In 1958 *Duncan* proved her excellent sea-keeping qualities in the tempestuous waters around Iceland during the first 'Cod War' of 1958–61. In reserve since 1972, she is retained as a harbour training vessel at HMS Caledonia, Rosyth.

Built: Thornycroft, Southampton (Dec. '53–Oct. '58). **Dimensions:** 310×33×11 ft = 1,180 tons. **Armament:** 2 triple Limbo DCMs; 4 21-in (twin) TTs; 3 40-mm (AA) guns. **Machinery:** 1-shaft steam turbines, 15,000 hp = 27¾ kts. **Boilers:** 2. **Fuel:** 275 tons oil. **Radius:** 4,000 mls at 12 kts. **Crew:** 140

Dewey (USA) 1958

World's first custom-built guided-missile armed surface vessel (as opposed to certain conversions and submarines) to enter service. Nine further ships of the Coontz class were completed between 1960–1. Designated frigates up to July 1975, they were then re-rated as destroyers. Their principal role is to provide AA cover for fast carrier groups.

The 5-in gun and Asroc 'pepper-box' launcher are carried forward of the bridge, while a twin launch ramp for 20-mile-range Terrier SAMs is mounted aft. Forty Terriers are fed automatically from their magazine to the firing position. These can intercept Mach 2+ targets to a ceiling of 65,000 feet. A helicopter landing area is sited aft.

Dewey was modernized in 1969–71, when her missile guidance equipment was up-dated.

Built: Bath Iron Works, Maine (Aug. '57–Dec. '59). **Dimensions:** $512\frac{1}{2} \times 52\frac{1}{2} \times 18$ ft = 4,700 tons. **Armament:** 1 twin Terrier SAM launcher, 1 octuple Asroc ASM launcher; 1 5-in (DP), 4 3-in (AA) guns; 6 12.75-in (triple) AS TTs. **Machinery:** 2-shaft steam turbines, 85,000 hp = 34 kts. **Boilers:** 4. **Crew:** 355

Otago (NZ) 1958

Originally ordered as HMS *Hastings*, a first-rate AS frigate of the Rothesay class. Her contract was taken over by the New Zealand Government in February 1957, who ordered a second unit, *Taranaki*, during the same month. Only minor alterations were made in the design to suit RNZN requirements, otherwise they are identical to Modified Type 12 frigates of the RN.

The 4.5-in guns are mounted in a twin turret forward, while two Limbo 3-barrelled DCMs are arranged aft, *en echelon*. Since completion, the single 40-mm gun sited abaft the funnel has been replaced by a quadruple Seacat SAM launcher.

Her excellent sea-keeping characteristics enable her to sustain high speed in all weathers. Fitted with two rudders to facilitate manœuvrability, she can be brought to a standstill from 30 knots in ninety seconds.

Built: Thornycroft, Southampton (Sept. '57–June '60). **Dimensions:** 370×41×12¾ ft = 2,144 tons. **Armament:** 2 4.5-in (DP), 1 40-mm (AA) guns; 12 21-in (AS) TTs; 2 triple Limbo DCMs. **Machinery:** 2-shaft steam turbines, 30,430 hp = 31 kts. **Boilers:** 2. **Fuel:** 370 tons oil. **Radius:** 4,500 mls at 12 kts. **Crew:** 240

Henry B. Wilson (USA) 1959

Second of twenty-three guided missile destroyers of the Charles F. Adams class to be commissioned into the USN during 1960–4. Six similar vessels were subsequently built in American yards, three each for the Federal German and Royal Australian Navies.

The two 5-in guns are fully automatic and radar-controlled, disposed in single turrets fore and aft, each with a sustained rate of fire of forty rounds per minute. Abaft the after 5-in mounting is a twin launch ramp for Mach 2 Tartar ship-to-air missiles, which are capable of a ten-mile slant range and of intercepting targets to a height of 40,000 feet. Forty-two Tartars are stowed in a below-decks magazine and fed direct to the launching position, enabling one missile to be aimed and fired every ten seconds.

Built: Defoe Sbdg, Michigan (Feb. '58–Dec. '60).
Dimensions: 437×47×15 ft = 3,370 tons.
Armament: 1 twin Tartar SAM launcher, 1 octuple Asroc ASM launcher; 2 5-in (DP) guns; 6 12.75-in (triple) AS TTs. **Machinery:** 2-shaft steam turbines, 70,000 hp = 35 kts. **Boilers:** 4. **Fuel:** 900 tons oil. **Radius:** 6,000/4,500/1,600 mls at 14/20/30 kts. **Crew:** 354

Long Beach (USA) 1959

World's first nuclear-powered surface vessel, and first major warship to be armed exclusively with guided missiles. However, two 5-in DP guns were subsequently fitted. Unlike earlier cruisers, *Long Beach* has no armour protection. Her missile armament comprises a twin launch ramp aft for Mach 2.5 Talos 65-mile-range SAMs (which also have an anti-ship capability), and two medium-range Terrier SAM systems forward. Talos and Terrier magazines can accommodate up to 46 and 120 missiles respectively. Talos missiles fired from USS *Long Beach* in the summer of 1968 destroyed two MiG fighters over North Vietnamese territory at a range of about 60 miles. These were the first 'kills' credited to ship-to-air missiles.

Long Beach's distinctive rectangular bridge structure incorporates a fixed-array of radar antennas ('billboards'), mounted on all four sides, which can achieve a greater range than rotating aerials. After four years' service and steaming 167,000 miles, she was refuelled, that is, fitted with new reactor cores, during her 1965–6 refit.

Built: Bethlehem Steel Co., Massachusetts (Dec. '57–Sept. '61). **Dimensions:** $721\frac{1}{4} \times 73\frac{1}{4} \times 29$ ft = 14,200 tons. **Armament:** 1 twin Talos SAM launcher, 2 twin Terrier SAM launchers, 1 octuple Asroc ASM launcher; 6 12.75-in (triple) AS TTs. **Machinery:** 2-shaft steam turbines, 80,000 hp = 35 kts. **Reactors:** 2. **Radius:** almost unlimited. **Crew:** 1,000

Enterprise (USA) 1960

First nuclear-powered aircraft carrier, and for the initial thirteen and a half years of her life had the added distinction of being the largest warship ever built. Her flight deck measures 257 feet at its widest point and covers an area of $4\frac{1}{2}$ acres. Two starboard elevators are positioned before the island and one abaft it. The fourth lift is sited on the port quarter.

The propulsion system consists of eight pressurized water-cooled nuclear reactors that provide steam to drive four sets of geared turbines, each of which subsequently turns a single propeller shaft. On her first set of reactor cores *Enterprise* steamed over 207,000 miles in three years; the second set achieved about 300,000 miles; while the third set is scheduled to last up to thirteen years.

To minimize construction costs ($451,300,000), no built-in armament was shipped, until two BPDMSs were installed in 1967 for close-range air defence while operating in the Gulf of Tonkin during the Vietnam War.

Built: Newport News, Virginia (Feb. '58–Nov. '61). **Dimensions:** 1,123×133 (fd: 257) ×$35\frac{3}{4}$ ft = 75,700 tons. **Armament:** 95 aircraft (4 catapults and 4 lifts). **Machinery:** 4-shaft steam turbines, 280,000 hp = 35 kts. **Reactors:** 8. **Radius:** almost unlimited. **Armour:** belt and flight deck. **Crew:** 5,500

Hamburg (D) 1960

First German destroyer of indigenous design to be built after WWII. Three sister ships, *Schleswig-Holstein*, *Bayern* and *Hessen*, were commissioned into the Bundesmarine in 1964, 1965 and 1968 respectively. Eight further units of the Staat class originally projected (some to have been armed with guided missiles) were deleted from the building programme in July 1958. The main armament, of French manufacture, is radar-controlled and disposed in four centreline turrets, superfiring fore and aft. Each 3.9-in gun is fully automatic, with a sustained rate of fire of sixty rounds per minute. Three 21-in torpedo tubes are built into the bow, with two more in the stern.

Built: H. C. Stülcken Sohn, Hamburg (1959–Mar. '64). **Dimensions:** $439\frac{3}{4} \times 44 \times 17$ ft = 3,340 tons. **Armament:** 4 3.9-in (DP), 8 40-mm (AA) guns; 8 375-mm (quadruple) AS rocked launchers, 1 DCT; 5 21-in (fixed) anti-ship, 2 12-in (single) AS TTs. **Machinery:** 2-shaft steam turbines, 68,000 hp = $35\frac{3}{4}$ kts. **Boilers:** 4. **Fuel:** 674 tons oil. **Radius:** 6,000/920 mls at 13/35 kts. **Crew:** 280

Iwo Jima (USA) 1960

First ship designed and built exclusively for helicopter operations. Six more amphibious assault ships of her class, *Okinawa*, *Guadalcanal*, *Guam*, *Tripoli*, *New Orleans* and *Inchon*, commissioned during 1962–70. Of relatively simple construction, they bear a marked resemblance to WWII escort carriers, although the flight deck and hangar are built into the hull girder.

Each ship can carry a Marine battalion landing team of 2,090 troops, together with its vehicles, artillery and other equipment, to virtually any trouble spot. These are ferried from ship to shore by two-dozen large transport helicopters to establish a beachhead. Thereafter they can be sustained for some considerable time or rapidly re-embarked. Casualties are treated in the vessel's own comprehensively equipped hospital.

Two deck-edge lifts connect the hangar and flight decks, one abaft the island, and one to port.

Built: Puget Sound N.Yd, Washington (Apr. '59– Aug. '61). **Dimensions:** 592×84 (fd:104)×26 ft = 17,000 tons. **Armament:** 28/32 helicopters (2 lifts); 8 3-in (AA) guns. **Machinery:** 1-shaft steam turbines, 23,000 hp = 22 kts. **Boilers:** 2. **Crew:** 528

Jeanne d'Arc (F) 1961

Represents a very interesting and highly original design, which can be readily employed as an AS helicopter carrier, a commando ship (with 700 fully equipped troops) or a command vessel, although her peace-time role is that of a training ship for officer cadets.

The flight deck measures $203\frac{1}{2} \times 69$ ft, below which is a spacious hangar. These are connected by an elevator positioned on the centreline aft, which can lift weights of up to twelve tons. Four large ASW helicopters are normally embarked, although in the event of war this figure would be doubled. After sea trials the funnel was substantially heightened to keep the bridge clear of smoke and exhaust fumes in a following wind. Lavish communication, surveillance and detection equipment are shipped, including long-range sonar, which augments the dipping variety carried by the ship's own helicopters.

Built: Naval Dockyard, Brest (July '60–June '64).
Dimensions: $597 \times 78\frac{3}{4} \times 21\frac{2}{3}$ ft = 10,000 tons.
Armament: 4/8 helicopters (1 lift); 43.9-in (DP) guns. **Machinery:** 2-shaft steam turbines, 40,000 hp = $26\frac{1}{2}$ kts. **Boilers:** 4. **Fuel:** 1,360 tons oil.
Radius: 6,000 mls at 15 kts. **Crew:** 906

London (GB) 1961

Guided-missile destroyer of the County class, of which eight units were completed during 1962–70. The term 'destroyer' is a misnomer when applied to vessels such as these, as they are comparable in size to many pre-war cruisers.

Mounted on the quarterdeck is the Seaslug launcher. This fires 24-mile-range, beam-riding missiles, which are capable of intercepting supersonic targets above 50,000 feet. Forward of this, at upper-deck level, are the flight deck and hangar for a Wessex helicopter (equipped with dipping sonar and homing torpedoes). Seacat SAM

systems are carried on each beam, with an effective range of about 2 miles. The radar-controlled 4.5-in guns are grouped forward in twin turrets.

The rest of the class comprises: *Devonshire, Hampshire, Kent, Fife, Glamorgan, Norfolk* and *Antrim.*

Built: Swan Hunter, Wallsend-on-Tyne (Feb. '60–Nov. '63). **Dimensions:** $520\frac{1}{2} \times 54 \times 16$ ft = 5,440 tons. **Armament:** 1 twin Seaslug SAM launcher, 2 quadruple Seacat SAM launchers; 4 4.5-in (DP) guns; 1 ASW helicopter. **Machinery:** 2-shaft steam+gas turbines, 60,000 hp = $32\frac{1}{2}$ kts. **Boilers:** 2. **Fuel:** 600 tons oil. **Crew:** 440

Caio Duilio   (I)   1962

Second of two Andrea Doria class guided-missile escort cruisers to be completed in 1964. Each vessel perpetuates the name of a former battleship which fought in both world wars.

Of versatile design, they are capable of performing both AA and AS duties. A high beam to length ratio for good stability makes these ships steady weapon platforms. For air defence a Terrier SAM launcher is mounted on the forecastle, which is backed up by a battery of eight quick-firing 3-in guns disposed four a side in single mountings.

A flight deck measuring $98\frac{1}{2} \times 52\frac{1}{2}$ ft is situated aft, from which four ASW helicopters operate.

The 12-in AS torpedoes are launched from a position abreast the fore end of the bridge, with triple banks of tubes on each side.

Built: Navalmeccanica Castellammare di Stabia (May '58–Nov. '64). **Dimensions:** $489\frac{3}{4} \times 56\frac{1}{3} \times 16\frac{1}{3}$ ft = 5,000 tons. **Armament:** 1 twin Terrier SAM launcher; 8 3-in (AA) guns; 6 12-in (triple) AS TTs; 4 ASW helicopters. **Machinery:** 2-shaft steam turbines, 60,000 hp = 31 kts. **Boilers:** 4. **Fuel:** 1,100 tons oil. **Radius:** 6,000 mls at 20 kts. **Crew:** 485

Zulu (GB) 1962

Frigate of the Tribal class, of which seven examples were completed during 1961–4. *Zulu* was preceded into service by *Ashanti, Tartar, Nubian, Gurkha, Eskimo* and *Mohawk*. Hitherto ships of this category had been designed for a specific role, for AS, AA or aircraft-direction duties. The Tribals, however, were built to perform all three functions, and were therefore classified as general-purpose frigates.

The COSAG propulsion system comprises a steam turbine for sustained cruising (developing up to 12,500 hp for $24\frac{3}{4}$ kts), and a gas turbine to provide an additional boost of 7,500 hp. The gas turbine can be used independently to get the vessel under way when the boilers are shut down.

These were the first frigates to be fitted with a hangar (sited between the Limbo and after 4.5-in gun) which is surmounted by the flight deck.

Built: Alex. Stephen, Glasgow (Dec. '60–Apr. '64). **Dimensions:** $360 \times 42\frac{1}{3} \times 11\frac{1}{4}$ ft = 2,300 tons. **Armament:** 2 4.5-in (DP) guns; 2 quadruple Seacat SAM launchers; 1 triple Limbo DCM; 1 ASW helicopter. **Machinery:** 1-shaft steam+gas turbines, 20,000 hp = 28 kts. **Boilers:** 1+1 auxiliary. **Fuel:** 400 tons oil. **Crew:** 253

Garcia (USA) 1963

Gives her name to a class of ten ships originally rated as ocean escorts but reclassified as frigates in July 1975.

Sited immediately before the bridge is the 'pepper-box' launcher for the Asroc system. This fires eight AS missiles, either singly or collectively, which follow a ballistic trajectory until reaching a computed position up to five miles from the launching point. An acoustic homing torpedo is then ejected in the proximity of the target. The flight deck and hangar aft were originally intended for two radio-controlled Drone Anti-Submarine Helicopters (DASH), each carrying a pair of homing torpedoes. *Garcia* never received DASH, because of its disappointing performance, but was subsequently provided with a conventional SH-2D Seasprite (LAMPS) ASW helicopter.

Built: Bethlehem Steel Co., California (Oct. '62–Dec. '64). **Dimensions:** $414\frac{1}{2} \times 44\frac{1}{4} \times 19$ ft = 2,620 tons. **Armament:** 1 octuple Asroc ASM launcher; 2 5-in (DP) guns; 6 12.75-in (triple) AS, 2 19-in (fixed) AS TTs; 2 DASH helicopters. **Machinery:** 1-shaft steam turbines, 35,000 hp = 27+ kts. **Boilers:** 2. **Crew:** 245

Kashin class (USSR) 1964

Designated by NATO the Kashin class, this group of destroyers were the first major combat vessels of any navy to nave all-gas-turbine propulsion, which offers rapid acceleration and instant availability of power, even when the ship is inert.

The main armament comprises two Goa SAM systems, for which double launchers are superimposed over the twin 3-in gun mountings fore and aft. This weapon is estimated to have a slant range of 15 miles, an operational ceiling of 44,000 ft, and a burn-out speed in the region of Mach 2.

The above photograph shows a member of the class, *Obraztsovy* during a courtesy visit to Portsmouth in May 1976. Nineteen Kashin class destroyers are reported to have been completed since 1962, one of which blew up and sank in the Black Sea in September 1974 with the loss of nearly 300 lives.

Built: Zhdanov Yard, Leningrad (Est. '63–Est. '66). **Dimensions:** $471 \times 52\frac{1}{2} \times 19$ ft = 4,300 tons. **Armament:** 2 twin Goa SAM launchers; 4 76-mm (DP) guns; 5 21-in (quintuple) AS TTs, 24 250-mm (AS), 12 300-mm (AS) rocket tubes. **Machinery:** 2-shaft gas turbines, 96,000 hp = 35 kts. **Crew:** 350

Juno (GB) 1965

General-purpose frigate of the Leander class, of which twenty-six units were completed during 1963–73. Representing nearly half the RN's current strength in this category, they are the largest group of major warships built to a single design for British service since WWII.

In addition to the hull-mounted sonar, VDS is carried at the stern. The mainmast is surmounted by a single bedstead aerial for Type 965 air-surveillance radar. The after section of the superstructure contains a hangar for the Wasp helicopter. This operates from a small flight deck near the stern, and is armed with a pair of homing torpedoes.

Most of the Leanders either have been or are scheduled to undergo modernization. *Juno* is to have her 4.5-in turret replaced by a quadruple Exocet SSM launcher. Others have received the Ikara ASM system, which delivers homing torpedoes up to 13 miles from its firing position.

Built: Thornycroft, Southampton (July '64–July '67). **Dimensions:** 372 × 41 × 13½ ft = 2,450 tons. **Armament:** 1 Seacat SAM launcher; 2 4.5-in (DP), 2 20-mm (AA) guns; 1 triple Limbo DCM; 1 ASW helicopter. **Machinery:** 2-shaft steam turbines, 30,000 hp = 30 kts. **Boilers:** 2. **Fuel:** 460 tons oil. **Radius:** 4,500 mls at 12 kts. **Crew:** 251

Kresta I class   (USSR)   1965

Dubbed the Kresta I class by NATO, the four ships of this group are designated large AS ships.

Twin launch ramps for Goa SAMs are disposed fore and aft, while double launchers (actually non-reloadable cylindrical containers) for Shaddock cruise missiles, are mounted on each side abreast the bridge structure. This weapon is credited with a maximum range of about 300 miles at transonic speed, although without some form of mid-course guidance its effective scope is probably limited to about 100 miles. However, the ASW helicopter may well fill this gap. The two 12-barrelled 250-mm AS rocket tubes are positioned on the forecastle, while a second pair of 6-tube 300-mm launchers is carried aft.

Built: Zhdanov Shipyard, Leningrad (Sept. '64–Feb. '67). **Dimensions:** 510×55×18 ft = 5,140 tons. **Armament:** 2 twin Goa SAM launchers, 2 twin Shaddock SSM launchers; 4 57-mm (DP) guns; 10 21-in (quintuple) TTs; 24 250-mm (AS), 12 300-mm (AS) rocket tubes; 1 ASW helicopter. **Machinery:** 2-shaft steam turbines, 100,000 hp = 34 kts. **Boilers:** 4. **Radius:** 4,500 mls at 18 kts. **Crew:** 400

Moskva (USSR) 1965

The appearance of this ship coinciding with the public unveiling of the Yakovlev 'Freehand' VTOL aircraft caused anxiety among Western naval observers, as these two factors suggested the Soviet Union's first tentative step towards the development of an aircraft carrier. Hitherto Russia had outwardly shown little interest in acquiring carriers. A second cruiser helicopter carrier, *Leningrad*, was commissioned in 1969.

The main armament is carried forward and comprises from the bow aft a twin-arm launcher for ASMs, and two superimposed double launch ramps for Goblet 20-mile-range SAMs, for which 180 reloads are provided. The large midship superstructure is topped by an oblique funnel, angled aft. Abaft this is a $295\frac{1}{4} \times 115$ ft flight deck.

Built: Nosenko Yard, Nikolayev (Est. '62–July '67). **Dimensions:** $644\frac{3}{4} \times 76 \times 25$ ft = 15,000 tons. **Armament:** 20 ASW helicopters (2 lifts); 2 twin Goblet SAM launchers, 1 twin ASM launcher; 4 57-mm (DP) guns; 24 250-mm (AS) rocket tubes; 10 21-in (quintuple) TTs. **Machinery:** 2-shaft steam turbines, 100,000 hp = 30 kts. **Boilers:** 4. **Crew:** 800

Carabiniere (I) 1967

Second and final frigate of the Alpino class, both ships being completed in 1968. Designed principally for an AS role, for which she is equipped with two Agusta-Bell 204B helicopters (each armed with a pair of homing torpedoes and dipping sonar). These are augmented by a single-barrelled DCM (sited between 'B' gun and the bridge), which can fire up to fifteen 12-in DCs per minute to a range in excess of 1,500 yards. In addition, triple banks of tubes for AS torpedoes are carried on each side. VDS is mounted at the stern. The 3-in guns are disposed in single mountings, two on the centreline before the bridge, and two on each side abreast the funnel and hangar structure.

Four sets of diesels can develop up to 16,800 hp for a speed of 22 knots, with an extra 15,000 hp being achieved from a pair of gas turbines for an additional 7 knots.

Built: Cantiere del Tirreno, Riva Trigoso (Jan. '65–Apr. '68). **Dimensions:** $371\frac{2}{3} \times 43\frac{1}{2} \times 12\frac{2}{3}$ ft = 2,420 tons. **Armament:** 6 3-in (DP) guns; 1 DCM; 6 12-in (triple) AS TTs; 2 ASW helicopters. **Machinery:** 2-shaft diesels+gas turbines, 31,800 hp = 29 kts. **Fuel:** 275 tons oil. **Radius:** 4,200 mls at 18 kts. **Crew:** 253

Amazon (GB) 1971

Gives her name to a new class of ultra-fast frigate, of which she was the prototype. She was the RN's first commercially designed warship since Thornycrofts built the two Brecon class frigates of 1942, from which *Amazon* derives certain features.

Amazon was the first major British warship to be built with all-gas-turbine machinery: this form of propulsion offers considerable savings in weight and space, reductions in manpower, and allows rapid replacement for maintenance purposes. The COGOG arrangement has been adopted, comprising two Tyne engines (8,000 hp) for sustained cruising, and two Olympus engines (a marine version of the type that powers the Concorde airliner) for attaining full speed. These two power sources are used independently and not together for boost.

Seven sister ships, *Antelope, Active, Ambuscade, Arrow, Alacrity, Ardent* and *Avenger*, are expected to be in service by 1979.

Built: Vosper Thornycroft, Southampton (Nov. '69–May '74). **Dimensions:** 384×41¾×12¼ ft = 2,500 tons. **Armament:** 1 4.5-in (DP), 2 20-mm (AA) guns; 1 quadruple Seacat SAM launcher; 6 12.75-in (triple) AS TTs; 1 ASW helicopter. **Machinery:** 2-shaft gas turbines, 56,000 hp = 35 kts. **Radius:** 4,500 mls at 18 kts. **Crew:** 170

Audace (I) 1971

And sister ship *Ardito*, constitute the Italian Navy's newest class of guided missile destroyer. *Audace* is seen here running sea trials, without her four midship 3-in guns, which have not yet been installed.

The 5-in guns are grouped forward in single fibre-glass turrets, each of which can fire up to forty-five rounds per minute. When fitted the 3-in battery will be disposed in single mountings, two on each side, and have a rate of fire of eighty-five rounds per barrel per minute. Both calibres are fully automatic and radar-controlled. The single-arm launcher for Tartar medium-range SAMs and its associated directors are mounted abaft the second funnel. Contained within the after super-structure is a hangar for two ASW helicopters, which operate from a small landing area on the quarterdeck. 21-in TTs are built into the stern.

Built: Cantieri del Tirreno, Riva Trigoso (Apr. '68–Nov. '72). **Dimensions:** $446\frac{1}{3} \times 47 \times 15$ ft = 3,600 tons. **Armament:** 1 single Tartar SAM launcher; 2 5-in (DP), 4 3-in (AA) guns; 6 12.75-in (triple) AS, 4 21-in (fixed) TTs; 2 ASW helicopters. **Machinery:** 2-shaft steam turbines, 73,000 hp = 33 kts. **Boilers:** 4. **Crew:** 380

Sheffield (GB) 1971

Prototype and name ship of Britain's latest class of guided-missile destroyer. Although less than half the size of her famous namesake (qv), she is potentially more effective than a WWII battleship.

The Sea Dart launcher is sited before the bridge, and fires 20-mile-range semi-active radar homing SAMs, which also possess an anti-ship capability. Forward of this is carried a fully automatic 4.5-in gun enclosed in a fibre-glass turret. Provided aft are a hangar and flight deck for the newly developed Lynx ASW helicopter, which will have the ability to fire Sea Skua air-to-surface missiles.

Fire more units of the class, *Birmingham*, *Coventry*, *Cardiff*, *Newcastle* and *Glasgow*, are due to join the fleet by 1979. A seventh ship, *Exeter*, has been ordered, while two more are being built for the Argentine Navy.

Built: Vickers, Barrow-in-Furness (Jan. '70–Feb. '75). **Dimensions:** 410×47×14 ft = 3,500 tons. **Armament:** 1 twin Sea Dart SAM launcher; 1 4.5-in (DP), 2 20-mm (AA) guns; 1 ASW helicopter. **Machinery:** 2-shaft gas turbines, 56,000 hp = 32 kts. **Radius:** 4,500 mls at 18 kts. **Crew:** 300

Colbert (F) 1972

First commissioned in May 1959 as an anti-aircraft cruiser of the improved De Grasse type. As such, her armament comprised sixteen 5-in DP and twenty 57-mm AA guns mounted in twin turrets, at five different levels.

After reconstruction all 5-in and eight 57-mm guns had been suppressed in favour of two rapid-fire 3.9-in guns in single turrets forward, and a Masurca SAM launcher (with its associated directors) aft. The latter fires 22-mile-range semi-active radar homing missiles, which achieve a speed of Mach 2.5 at burn-out. Forty-eight Masurca missiles are stowed in a below-decks magazine.

In addition to her primary role, *Colbert* was originally designed to serve as a command ship, a radar direction vessel (controlling air strikes by carrier-borne and shore-based aircraft), or in an emergency to act as a fast transport with accommodation for up to 2,400 fully equipped troops.

Converted: Naval Dockyard, Brest (Apr. '70–Oct. '72). **Dimensions:** $593\frac{1}{4} \times 64\frac{2}{3} \times 21\frac{3}{4}$ ft = 8,500 tons. **Armament:** 1 twin Masurca SAM launcher; 2 3.9-in (DP), 12 57-mm (AA) guns. **Machinery:** 2-shaft steam turbines, 86,000 hp = $32\frac{1}{2}$ kts. **Boilers:** 4. **Fuel:** 1,492 tons oil. **Radius:** 4,000 mls at 25 kts. **Armour:** belt 3 in, deck 2 in. **Crew:** 796

Kiev (USSR) 1972

Largest warship ever built in Russia and the Soviet Navy's first aircraft carrier. She was officially classified as an anti-submarine cruiser, possibly in order to circumvent a clause in the Montreux Convention of July 1936 regarding the passage of aircraft carriers through the Turkish Straits; she infringed this when passing through the Bosporus from her builders in the Black Sea to the Mediterranean in July 1976.

Kiev differs radically from the *Moskva* design, with her large island superstructure on the starboard side, which leaves her angled flight deck of about 600 feet in length completely unobstructed. This provides her Yak-36 VTOL fighters (evolved from the 'Freehand' research aircraft) with a short take-off run, which enables a greater payload to be carried while burning a lot less fuel.

A sister ship, *Minsk*, is now fitting out at Nikolayev, while a further unit is being built at the same yard. Others are expected to follow.

Built: Nosenko Yard, Nikolayev (Est. '70–July '76). **Dimensions:** 925×100(fd: 200)×30 ft = 35,000 tons. **Armament:** 15 aircraft+20 ASW helicopters (2 lifts); 1 twin ASM launcher, 2 twin Goblet SAM launchers, 4 twin (SAN-4) SAM launchers, 4 twin (SSN-10) SSM launchers; 4 76-mm (DP), 8 30-mm (AA) guns; 24 250-mm (AS) rocket tubes. **Machinery:** 4-shaft gas turbines, 212,000 hp = 33 kts. **Crew:** 2,000

Nimitz (USA) 1972

World's largest warship, and the USN's second nuclear-powered aircraft carrier. Owing to the great strides made in nuclear technology during the ten years between the preparation of designs for *Nimitz* and *Enterprise*, only two reactors were required for the former's power plant instead of eight. The first pair of reactor cores installed in this ship are estimated to produce enough energy for her to steam up to 1 million miles (equal to 1,620,000 tons of fuel oil), without refuelling.

Close-range aerial defence is in the form of three BPDMSs, mounted on sponsons on the starboard bow and each side aft. These fire 7-mile-range Sea Sparrow SAMs.

Two sister ships, *Dwight D. Eisenhower* and *Carl Vinson*, are scheduled for completion in 1977 and 1981 respectively.

Built: Newport News, Virginia (June '68—May '75). **Dimensions:** 1,092×134(fd: 252)×37 ft = 81,600 tons. **Armament:** 95 aircraft (4 catapults and 4 lifts); 3 octuple Sea Sparrow SAM launchers. **Machinery:** 4-shaft steam turbines, 260,000 hp = 30+ kts. **Reactors:** 2. **Radius:** almost unlimited. **Crew:** 6,100

Tiger (GB) 1972

Has had a remarkably chequered building and service history. Launched in October 1945, as a Minotaur class cruiser. Work was suspended from July 1946. Laid up until 1954 when she was partially dismantled for completion in 1959 to a revised design, with four 6-in and six 3-in guns.

In December 1966 *Tiger* was the venue for the first round of abortive talks between the British Prime Minister (Harold Wilson) and the Rhodesian leader (Ian Smith), over Rhodesia's future.

On conversion to a command helicopter cruiser, *Tiger*'s after 6-in turret was removed to enable a large hangar and flight deck to be built aft, while her midship 3-in turrets were replaced by two Seacat SAM systems.

Converted: HM Dockyard, Devonport (1968–May '72). **Dimensions:** $566\frac{1}{2} \times 64 \times 18$ ft = 9,500 tons. **Armament:** 2 6-in (DP), 2 3-in (DP) guns; 2 quadruple Seacat SAM launchers; 4 Sea King ASW helicopters. **Machinery:** 4-shaft steam turbines, 80,000 hp = $31\frac{1}{2}$ kts. **Boilers:** 4. **Fuel:** 1,850 tons oil. **Radius:** 6,500/4,000/2,000 mls at 13/20/30 kts. **Armour:** belt $3\frac{1}{2}$ in, turrets 3 in, deck 2 in. **Crew:** 885

Storozhevoy (USSR) 1973

Belongs to the Soviet Navy's most recent class of guided-missile destroyer, of which about eleven have so far been completed. These are known in the West by the NATO code-name of Krivak class. The existence of these ships became known to Western naval intelligence in 1971. They have replaced the Kashin class in production, with a building rate of about two per year. Gas-turbine propulsion, combined with their excellent hull design, renders these destroyers potentially the fastest of their kind anywhere in the world today.

A quadruple launcher for 29-mile-range SSMs is carried on the forecastle. Mounted before the bridge and abaft the funnel are two retractable twin-arm launchers for 20-mile-range SAMs. After firing these are lowered through the deck for re-loading or, when not in use, are retained in the lowered position for stowage as protection against the elements. Quadruple banks of 21-in TTs are mounted on each side amidships, while two sets of twelve 250-mm AS rocket tubes are carried immediately forward of the bridge. The four 76-mm guns are disposed in twin turrets in a superfiring arrangement aft. VDS is fitted, in addition to bow-mounted sonar.

Dimensions: $404\frac{3}{4} \times 46 \times 16\frac{1}{2}$ ft = 3,500 tons. **Armament:** 1 quadruple (SSN-10) SSM launcher, 2 twin (SAN-4) SAM launchers; 4 76-mm (DP), 4 30-mm (AA) guns; 8 21-in (quadruple) AS TTs; 24 250-mm (AS) rocket tubes. **Machinery:** 2-shaft gas turbines, 112,000 hp = 38 kts.

Invincible (GB) 1977

The lead and name ship of a class of three so-called 'through-deck cruisers', which are in fact more akin to light fleet aircraft carriers.

Invincible is the largest warship to be built in Britain for more than thirty years. Two centreline lifts will connect the hangar and flight decks. It is anticipated that her single-storeyed hangar will have sufficient capacity for at least five Sea Harrier VTOL fighters and ten large Sea King ASW helicopters. A twin Sea Dart launcher for 20-mile-range SAMs will be mounted on the forecastle, forward of the slightly angled flight deck.

The most distinctive feature of this class will be the very long (in relation to the total length) starboard-sided island superstructure, with its two funnel and mast arrangement. The primary role of these ships will be ASW, although they will also be employed as command ships, and to provide air cover for the fleet.

The second ship of the class (ordered 1976) is to be named *Illustrious*. A third unit is projected.

Built: Vickers, Barrow-in-Furness (July '73– Est. '81). **Dimensions:** 677×90 (fd: 104½) × 24 ft = 20,000 tons. **Armament:** 5 aircraft+10 helicopters (2 lifts); 1 twin Sea Dart SAM launcher. **Machinery:** 2-shaft gas turbines, 112,000 hp = 30 kts. **Radius:** 5,000 mls at 18 kts. **Crew:** 1,000

Acknowledgments

The author and publishers would like to thank the following for their generous help in providing illustrations for this book:

Department of National Defence, Ottawa, Canada: *79, 94*
Etablissement Cinématographique et Photographique des Armées (France): *95, 104, 117*
Federal German Navy: *102*
Harland and Wolff Limited: *60, 84*
Italian Navy: *7, 27, 59, 93, 106, 113, 115*
Ministry of Defence (Royal Navy): *86, 107, 109, 116, 119, 121, 123*
Royal Netherlands Navy: *78, 90*
Royal New Zealand Navy: *50, 98*
Scott-Lithgow Limited: *40*
Swan Hunter Group Limited: *105*
US Navy: *2, 15, 43, 51, 58, 62, 66, 69 (below), 70, 71, 73, 75, 77, 81, 91, 92, 97, 99, 100, 101, 103, 108, 111, 112, 120*
Vickers Limited: *18, 20, 28, 29, 32, 47, 55, 57, 64, 67, 74, 89, 124*
Vosper Thornycroft Limited: *46, 87, 96, 110, 114*
Yarrow (Shipbuilders) Limited: *61, 76*

Additional photographs supplied by:
Imperial War Museum: *9, 14, 19, 21, 22, 23, 24, 25, 26, 30, 33, 34, 39, 42, 44, 63, 65, 69 (top)*
Wright and Logan, Portsmouth: *11, 13, 31, 35, 36, 37, 38, 41, 45, 49, 52, 53, 54, 56, 80, 82, 83, 85, 88*

Index